THE BATTLE
OF WATERLOO

THE MACMILLAN BATTLE BOOKS
are prepared under the general editorship of
Edward R. Sammis

Special maps drawn by Harry Rosenbaum

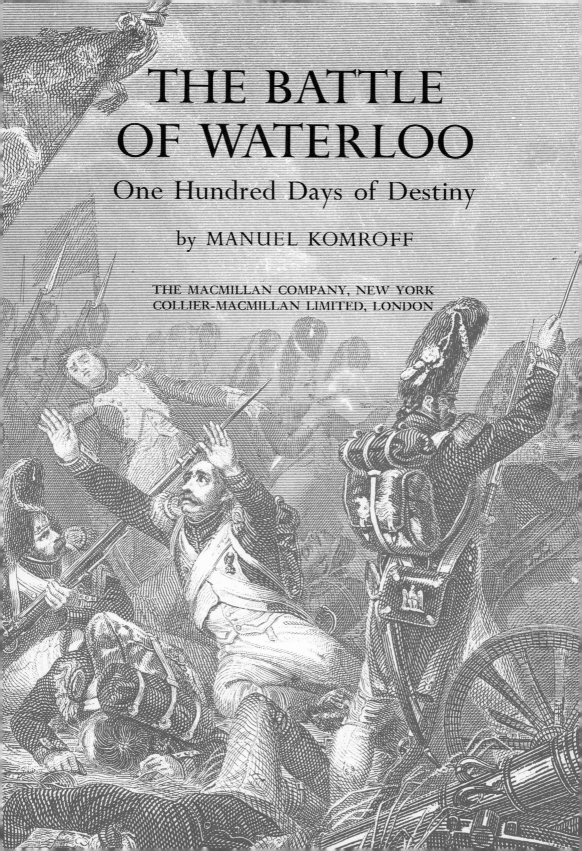

THE BATTLE OF WATERLOO

One Hundred Days of Destiny

by MANUEL KOMROFF

THE MACMILLAN COMPANY, NEW YORK
COLLIER-MACMILLAN LIMITED, LONDON

CONTENTS

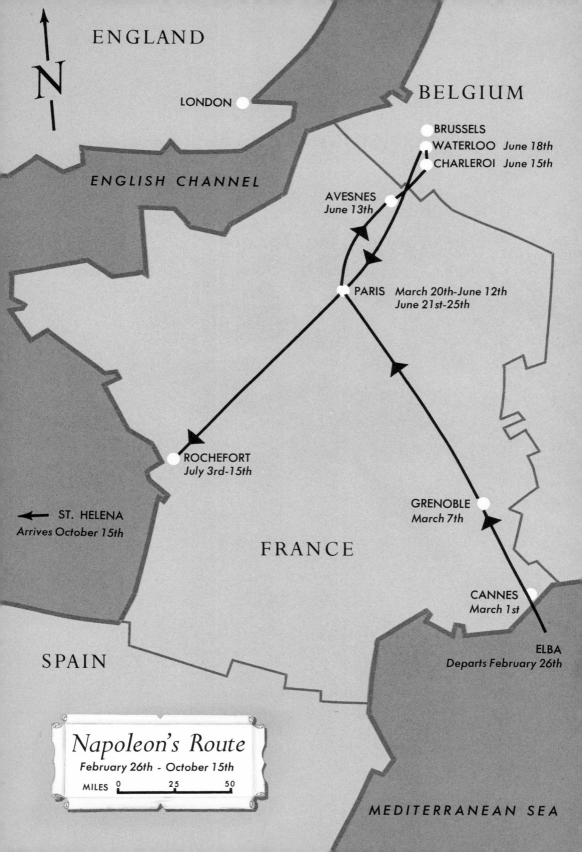

PART ONE

THE EXILE RETURNS

On a winding road in the south of France, early in the spring of the year 1815, two bodies of marching men rapidly approached each other. Then, when they were only a few yards apart, they stopped.

The two groups could hardly have been in sharper contrast: On the one side, the spruce, elegantly uniformed soldiers of the King's guard; on the other, a rag-and-bobtail horde, some wearing the faded uniforms of old campaigns, some still in their peasant blouses, just as they had come from the fields.

This was a tense moment.

The commander of the King's Fifth Regiment had his orders from the monarch himself: "Bring back Napoleon in an iron cage." And now Napoleon, riding on a white horse at the head of his outlaws, loomed before him.

The soldiers of the King faced a man they well remembered. For twenty years he had been their master. Many of them had marched under him in campaigns history would never forget, as the mightiest military forces in the world had trembled before the "Little Corsican." Finally, after the disastrous Russian campaign he had been beaten. France had been invaded, Napoleon driven into exile on the tiny Mediterranean island of Elba, and King Louis XVIII restored to the throne.

A few days before, Napoleon had returned to France. Landing near Cannes on the southern coast, he had begun his march up the road to Grenoble. Compared to the great armies he had once commanded, his army was now a tiny one, but fanatically loyal.

At this moment his soldiers faced their first test. Would the Fifth Regiment be able to stop them?

On the road to Paris, Napoleon Bonaparte shrewdly plays upon the sentiments of soldiers in the King's Fifth Regiment, knowing that with the simplest speech he can sway them to defect to him.

Sitting astride his horse, Napoleon looked at the King's men sent to seize him, and smiled. Across the few yards of road, two rows of soldiers leveled their muskets at each other. Who would fire the first shot?

With a characteristically bold gesture, Napoleon got down from his horse and swaggered out into the dusty stretch between the hostile forces. Then something incredible happened: He was unbuttoning his coat! Defiantly, he flung it open and offered his chest to the King's bullets.

"Soldiers of the Fifth Regiment!" he called out. "Do you not recognize me?" An awful stillness hung over the scene. He stood without moving, his coat still held open. Then he shouted, "If anyone wants to kill me, then let him do so!"

The King's commander gave the order to his men: "FIRE!"

Not a shot rang out. Suddenly from the King's soldiers a mighty cheer arose. "Long live the Emperor!" As one man, they placed their caps on the tips of their bayonets and raised them aloft. A new shout went up: "Down with the Royalists!" Then, they rushed to join Napoleon's forces. The King's soldiers, being men of the people, secretly hated aristocrats, and especially the King. Among themselves, they called him "Louis the Pig."

With redoubled forces, Napoleon Bonaparte marched on.

The Congress of Vienna

Meanwhile, in the grand ballrooms of Vienna, one of the most brilliant social assemblages in history was being held. From every corner of Europe emperors, kings, princes, noblemen, and diplomats had come to dance the Vienna waltzes—and between parties to carve up the pie of Europe for themselves, now that Napoleon was defeated.

Whether for political or social reasons, the Congress of Vienna in March, 1815, attracted most of the conservative rulers of Europe, many of them powerful, but all of them blind to the real threat of the "Little Corsican," then well on his way to Paris.

News traveled slowly in those days. Napoleon was already marching through southern France, gathering forces as he went, when the latest couriers reaching Vienna brought tidings that the former scourge of Europe was still safely imprisoned on the island of Elba. There, so the rumors went, he played cards every night, and pretended to be ruler over a little mock court of his fellow prisoners. The diplomats laughed, lulled by this news into a feeling of false security, and went on with their dancing.

Vienna was the hub of the Austro-Hungarian Empire.

With its lavish palaces, its love of gaiety and music, it was also the social capital of the Western world. The rulers gathered there had wished chiefly to turn back the clock. They ignored as a temporary inconvenience the liberties and human rights which the French Revolution had established and which Bonaparte, without really intending to, had, by his conquests, spread in the minds of many of the people of Europe. These conservative rulers laughed at the idea of equality, convinced that their privileges belonged to them by a divine right. Among them were many powerful leaders: Alexander, the absolute ruler of Russia; the clubfooted Talleyrand of France; the crafty Metternich of Austria; a representative from clever Pope Pius VII; and, from England, the Duke of Wellington, a famous commander whose armies were still in Belgium after having helped to defeat the French.

The element of surprise had always been one of Napoleon's most effective weapons, and never had it worked better than it did now. By the time the news of his escape reached Vienna, he had been on French soil a full week. Suddenly the dancing stopped. Every ruler and diplomat in Vienna was stunned. Now they must unite if they were to be victorious against Napoleon. But they faced the same difficulty which had weakened them during the twenty years of Napoleon's rule: they were all torn by grave suspicions of each other. Now, instead of uniting, they fell to bickering. Unable to agree on what to do, they took refuge in wishful thinking. For the second time they lulled themselves into a false security by telling themselves that Louis XVIII would quickly capture the "little upstart" and throw him into a dungeon. Even the quiet, cautious Duke of Wellington sent this dispatch to London: "The King of France will destroy Napoleon without difficulty and in a short time."

The Escape

But, as before, his enemies underestimated Napoleon. In the long months of his exile on Elba, he had laid his plans carefully. His loyal supporters in Grenoble, a French glove-making town near the Swiss border, sent him messages hidden in the fingers of gloves. His followers adopted a secret slogan to prepare for his return in March: "The violets will bloom in the spring."

On the night of February 26, 1815, when the English governor of Elba was away on a holiday, the famous refugee had made his escape on the brig *Inconstant* with a thousand men and boatloads of supplies. Standing on deck in the famous stance with his hand between the buttons of his coat, he announced, "The die is cast." Then he went into the cabin and summoned his secretary. "A proclamation to the army," commanded Napoleon. "Write as I dictate." Pacing up and down the cabin floor, he spoke with as much eloquence as though he already stood before his troops. "Soldiers, we have not been conquered! In my exile I have heard your voice. And I have returned in spite of all obstacles and dangers. Your general . . . is restored to you. Come join him. . . . Take up those Eagles which you carried through our many victories . . . which brought glory to our country."

On March 1st, at a spot near Cannes, Napoleon stepped ashore on the southern coast of France.

The Road to Paris

He headed first for Grenoble, where he could count on the greatest support. To evade the King's forces, he took a roundabout road skirting the French Alps. At every village

Louis XVIII of France, 1775–1824 (Portrait by Baron Gérard)

his proclamation was read. Excitement spread throughout the countryside. Men, women, and children, loving him and hating the King, came forward to cheer, to follow his army, to sing songs against Louis. The ranks swelled. Many old veterans left their farms to march again under the Eagles of the Emperor.

After that moment on the road to Grenoble when the King's troops refused to fire on Napoleon, and joined him instead, he had a real fighting force.

His growing band reached the town in the evening. The city gates were locked; cannons threatened him from the walls. But his troops smashed the gates and poured in. A garrison of the King's soldiers was on guard at Grenoble, but, at the sight of Napoleon, they tore from their hats the white cockade—the symbol of Louis—and joined Napoleon's ranks. Mobs of peasants from nearby villages swarmed after them, and there was a grand torchlight parade. All night long shouts of "Long live the Emperor" and "Down with the Royalists" echoed through the streets. Of this night Napoleon was to say, "Until I reached Grenoble, I was an adventurer. At Grenoble I became a prince."

He marched on toward Paris. The enthusiasm was contagious; it swept the countryside like wind-whipped flame. Leading 7,000 troops, he took Lyon, the first city on his way to Paris, without a shot. More and more veterans who had fought under his banner from Spain to Moscow returned to his ranks, which mounted to 14,000, and then to an impressive 20,000.

In Paris, King Louis summoned redheaded Marshal Michel Ney, known as "the bravest of the brave," who had served under Napoleon, and gave him his orders. He was to mount a force against his old commander in chief. Ney willingly

On March 7, 1815, while on his way to Paris, Napoleon is welcomed by the citizens of Grenoble. (Painting by Hugues Merle)

swore allegiance to Louis XVIII. "I will arrest the adventurer," he said, "and bring him to Paris in an iron cage."

But as Ney led the King's troops to seize Napoleon, his allegiance wavered. He was basically suspicious of all aristocrats, particularly Louis and the other members of the Bourbon family. Also, the sentiment of the troops lay not with the King, but with Bonaparte. Ney feared that they would desert like the other Royalist soldiers Bonaparte had encountered. Nevertheless, he had sworn. Then he received a personal letter from Napoleon. In the familiar hand of his old commander, Ney read the words that proved a masterpiece of diplomacy: "Come to me, and I shall embrace you as I did after the Battle of Moskva!"

The Battle of Moskva, also known as the Battle of Borodino, had been a bloody one, fought in 1812 on the way to Moscow. After it, Napoleon had bestowed upon Ney the title "Prince of Moskva"; a week later the two men had entered the Kremlin together.

Ney was deeply moved by the letter. He weighed the question in his heart. Finally he called his officers together and announced, "The cause of the Bourbons is lost forever!" A hush fell over the circle. Then a grand cheer went up. "Long live the Emperor!" cried the officers, as Ney rode away to receive the promised embrace.

When Louis got word of Ney's defection, he fled hastily to Belgium. Now, for Napoleon the road to Paris was clear. He rode straight to the palace at the Tuileries, in the very heart of Paris. It was a dark, foggy night when he arrived, but the light from the crystal chandeliers glimmered in the tall windows: his friends were there to welcome him. Twenty days after setting foot on French soil, Napoleon was back in the palace. What did the rulers of Europe, dancing at

Vienna, matter to him now? Contemptuously, Napoleon announced to the world, "The Congress of Vienna is dissolved!"

When word reached the Congress that Napoleon had entered Paris without firing a shot, the group of rulers and diplomats was indeed dissolved. Those who had blinded themselves with the comfortable belief that Louis would soon capture the escaped prisoner were now seized with terror. Before disbanding, the members of the Congress issued a unanimous declaration of war, condemning Napoleon as an outlaw and "an enemy and disturber of the peace of the world." They rode off hurriedly in their carriages to their respective kingdoms. The Duke of Wellington left by fast coach to join his armies in Belgium.

Napoleon Consolidates His Power

The men who had just made the long march with Napoleon were weary. Their horses, tied to the railings surrounding the palace, nodded, and the soldiers slept on the ground beside them. But Napoleon did not sleep. Exhilarated by his return to power, he decided to waste no time. War was inevitable; he must prepare for it.

So, after the hastiest of greetings to his friends, he began dispatching messengers. Many of the ablest men in France were awakened in the middle of the night and summoned with great speed to the palace. The restored Emperor was making his appointments to key positions in the new Empire.

First, he asked Marshal Louis Nicolas Davout to serve as Minister of War. When Davout hesitated to accept, Napoleon used tactful but firm persuasion. Ten minutes later Davout was at his desk.

Napoleon then informed another faithful officer, Count Pierre-François Real, that he was to be the new Prefect of Police. The count accepted immediately, with the words, "I shall be there tomorrow morning." Napoleon replied, "You will go tonight." And he did.

For the next days, Napoleon worked without respite. He took only his famous brief naps. In the midst of a turmoil of interviews and conferences, he found time to write a long series of letters to his consort, Marie Louise, who was far away in Vienna. But Napoleon wrote: "I am once again master of France. The people and the army are wild with

On March 20th, Napoleon returns triumphantly to the palace at the Tuileries in Paris. (Engraving by Couché, after Heim)

enthusiasm! No one except the so-called King has run away. . . . I expect you here in April with my son."

Napoleon's little son, l'Aiglon, the Eaglet, was four years old the day his father marched into Paris. Loving him dearly, Napoleon had bestowed upon him the title, "King of Rome."

Peace and Freedom

Tense with anticipation, Napoleon paced back and forth in the vast rooms of the palace. Yes, he was again ruler of France. Yes, war was again imminent. Yes, his ministers and commanders were loyal. Another series of victories, and Europe would once more be groveling at his feet.

But he was worried, too. He sensed something different in the temper of his people. They no longer responded unreservedly, as they once had, to his leadership. What was wrong? He summoned an adviser. We may imagine the scene that followed:

"The people are infected with the ideas of democracy," the adviser informed him. "They still have affection for you, but they want freedom. They do not want to be dictated to."

"Democracy is nothing but mob rule," said Napoleon scornfully.

"Nevertheless, sir, it has a grip on the people."

"Why do they not volunteer for the French Army as they once did?"

"They want peace, sir. Above all, the women."

"Are they then so weak-kneed that they listen to women's talk when I offer them the promise of new victories, new glories for France?"

"Sir, they speak of the million men lost on the hot deserts of Egypt, the frozen plains of Russia, and the far-flung battlefields of Europe. France is weary of war, they say."

"Leave me."

"Thank you, sir."

Napoleon paced back and forth. He wore no smile now, but rather a dark frown. The people's sentiments meant nothing to him personally, but without their support he could not reassert his power. And yet it was imperative for him to fight and to fight soon. Great Britain, Prussia, Austria, and Russia had pooled 600,000 men, a force they pledged to maintain "until Bonaparte should have been rendered absolutely incapable of stirring up further trouble." In France men were not only failing to volunteer; they were even defying the draft, which, as free men, they said was unjust.

There was only one thing to do. Napoleon decided to feign a love for democracy and peace. He would speak softly to the people of France in order to win their hearts. Once he had done that, he would be able to appear once more as their absolute master, to make them believe that a strong army militarism was in their best interests as Frenchmen. So now the foundation was laid for a new kind of strategy.

Napoleon announced to the people that he sought no personal power, but that he had returned only because "things are not well with France." Then he told them the very opposite of what he really had in mind: "I do not want to carry on any more wars. We must forget that we are masters of the world. . . . We will work now for France's consolidation and tranquillity. . . ." He posed as the champion of the rights of man and the upholder of liberty. He promised the people free elections and a free press, and he consented to a liberal constitution and a government made up of an Upper and Lower House.

He carried through with these promises. Secretly he in-

Napoleon II (l'Aiglon), 1811–1832

Marie Louise, 1791–1847

tended to dissolve both Houses after his first victory, and to re-establish himself as a military dictator over all of France. But thus was born the First Republic.

The Champ de Mai

Napoleon's plan did not work perfectly, but the granting of various liberties did soften his image in the eyes of the people. Now to the thought that he had come as their "defender and protector," he added the idea "The country is in danger!" Again and again he repeated the warning that enemies were about to strike, and that they must be hurled back before they set foot on the sacred ground of France. In this way Napoleon was able to stir up extreme nationalism, that blind fever he knew would make people give up their new-found dignity to join the army. The shrewd Emperor, himself wishing to be an aristocrat, convinced many that equality and brotherhood could be furthered by militarism.

But Napoleon still needed many more volunteers than were signing up. He planned a huge public spectacle, a revival of a traditional spring festival dating back to the time of Charlemagne, called the *Champ de Mai*. Although supposedly to mark the adoption of the new constitution, the real purpose of this spectacle was to inflame the people's devotion to the nation and to Napoleon. He had great hopes that Marie Louise and l'Aiglon would be in Paris for the ceremony. Before the huge crowd that was anticipated, he planned to crown Marie Louise Empress. But when the great day came, neither she nor his son had arrived.

Napoleon tried to appear as regal as possible for the event. He reached the scene enveloped in an elaborate court costume, including a heavy ermine coronation mantle and a large hat with ostrich plumes, and riding in a coronation coach drawn by eight white horses. Having taken lessons in kingly deportment from the famous tragedian, François Joseph Talma, he did everything with highly artificial stage gestures. All of this was calculated to awe the people.

But they were still in a democratic mood. They were not impressed by the display. They had expected the "defender of France" to appear in his familiar old green military coat. A few onlookers even laughed at him.

The seasoned military man was not easily abashed, however. With his masterly sense of showmanship, Napoleon rose to address his subjects. Swearing to uphold the constitution, he first read that document. Then came his speech. It began with the words, "Emperor, Consul, and soldier, I owe all that I hold to the people." Many began to be swayed. As the speech went along, patriotic fervor rose in the crowd.

Afterward, Napoleon presented to each of his regiments its new flag. As each one swore its allegiance to the restored Empire, thousands of voices joined wildly in reply, with the words, "We swear it!"

Feeling the frenzy of nationalist pride mounting, Napoleon grew bolder. He spoke again of the ring of enemies surrounding the country. Then, flanked by 40,000 soldiers and 600 massed French tricolored flags, he spoke of what had been uppermost in his mind all along: the campaign that was about to begin.

By this time many Frenchmen were once more ready to die at the Emperor's orders. Many of the strong-willed still held out, however; for even Napoleon could not erase the weariness and horror of war so fresh in many memories.

Battle Plans

But war was now a certainty.

France had once raised a million men to kill and be killed at Napoleon's orders. Now, despite all his efforts to rouse the people, when he asked for 700,000 men, France had given him 400,000. And of these only 200,000 were properly equipped, with a mere 125,000 really ready for battle.

Very soon the rulers of Europe who had declared him an outlaw would force him to fight. Could he wait until it happened? This would mean that France herself must be the battleground. And it would mean his outnumbered army would have to defend itself on virtually every border. Even Spain and Switzerland had declared themselves against Napoleon. And on the defenseless eastern border, the Austrians and Russians were already mounting an attack. No, a defensive war was impossible.

During the Champ de Mai, *Napoleon publicly swears to uphold a constitution which he privately detests. (Drawing by Martinèt)*

He must attack. The enemy stronghold was Belgium, where the forces of the British Wellington and the German Gebhard von Blücher were spread over the area between Brussels and the French border. Every day those forces grew stronger; therefore delay was out of the question. It was necessary to attack immediately.

Also, victory in Belgium would fit perfectly into Napoleon's ambitious schemes at home. After the Revolution, Belgium had been French until it was captured by Napoleon's enemies. If he could again make Belgium part of France, this would touch the pride of the nation. He would come home a hero. The people's hearts would be solidly his again, and he could recruit a larger force to begin his career anew; the lust for military power would again have seized France.

The Road to Brussels

Napoleon worked out his strategy. He faced two great armies. Together, Wellington's forces and those of Blücher's Prussians outnumbered his, but separately they did not. The main bodies of their troops were located some distance apart. So Napoleon planned to wedge his forces between them and, dividing them from each other, strike at both from the center. He would hurl all his strength against one, and, when that one was defeated, swing about and annihilate the other.

Napoleon knew that this would be a most dangerous maneuver, for it would place his army between two powerful enemies who might unite to crush him in a pincers movement. But he had successfully used this form of attack before and was confident it would work.

He weighed the situation carefully. The more he thought about the odds, the more they seemed to be in his favor.

The fact that the two armies were separated and under different commands was a great advantage to him. True, they were united by a common interest: his total defeat. But in all other important ways they were divided. For one thing, the supply lines for the two armies lay in opposite directions. Wellington depended on the English Channel to the west, while Blücher's base of supply was the Rhineland to the east.

And the two generals and their troops differed greatly. Blücher was impulsive, haughty, overconfident. Only a year before, in January, 1814, when the Prussian invaded France, Napoleon had beaten him five times on five different fronts— and in two weeks! Napoleon had often boasted that one French fighting man was the equal of two Dutch or German soldiers. Knowing that the German general was quick to accept a challenge, Napoleon decided to attack Blücher first.

With Blücher beaten, he would turn and attack Wellington. Wellington's characteristics also fitted neatly into this plan. He was a careful, reserved, calculating man. He never rushed into battle until he was completely ready. This would give Napoleon time to reorganize after the battle with Blücher. There was another advantage: two-thirds of Wellington's army was made up of untrained Dutch, Belgian, and German mercenary troops. Some of these were old, no longer anxious to return to battle; the rest were raw recruits. Wellington would have to rely primarily on a small, tough force of seasoned British and Hanoverian soldiers.

Working late into the night, Napoleon pondered over his plan. Memories of his former glories rose in his mind. He burned with the desire to be back on the battlefield and to be a conqueror once more. And he was convinced his plan would work.

He summoned his aides.

In the very center of the enemies' southern line, at a town called Charleroi, there was a gap in their combined defenses along the French-Belgian border. From here, the main road led north through the villages of Quatre Bras and Waterloo to Brussels, the capital. But if Wellington, the Supreme Allied Commander, were to learn that French troops were moving toward this gap, he would have plenty of time to close it. Therefore secrecy was all important. Napoleon must take Wellington and the Prussian General Blücher by surprise, or they would unite their forces and he would be outnumbered two to one.

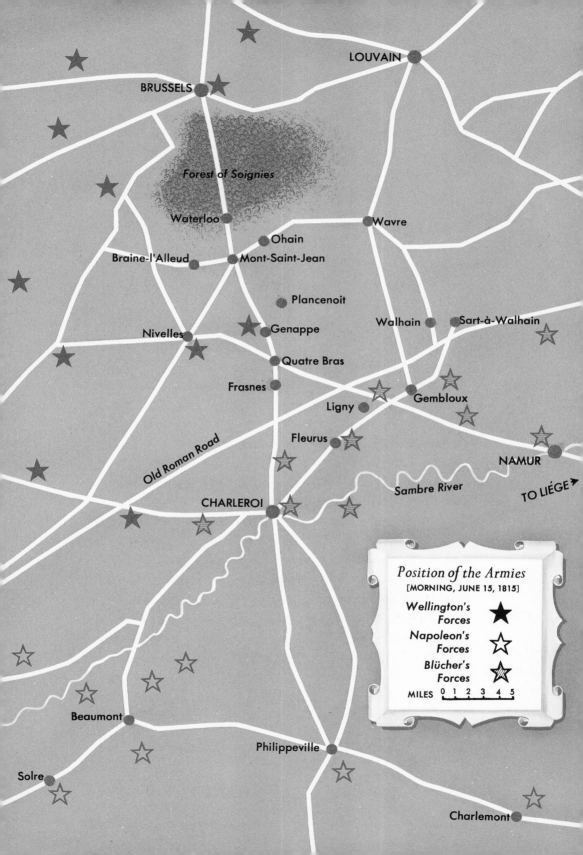

LOUVAIN

BRUSSELS

Forest of Soignies

Waterloo

Wavre

Ohain

Braine-l'Alleud   Mont-Saint-Jean

Plancenoit

Walhain   Sart-à-Walhain

Nivelles   Genappe

Quatre Bras

Frasnes   Ligny   Gembloux

Fleurus   NAMUR

Old Roman Road   Sambre River   TO LIÉGE ▶

CHARLEROI

Beaumont

Solre   Philippeville

Charlemont

Position of the Armies
[MORNING, JUNE 15, 1815]

Wellington's
Forces   ★

Napoleon's
Forces   ☆

Blücher's
Forces   ✮

MILES   0 1 2 3 4 5

PART TWO

THE PRECIOUS HOURS

"To Conquer or Die"

Secrecy and speed marked Napoleon's opening moves. He ordered the French forces, now scattered between Paris and the Belgian border, to march at once. Concealing their movements, they were to convene within three days on the French side of the border at Beaumont, Solre, and Philippeville.

Napoleon himself left Paris near midnight on June 11th. He reached his troops on the evening of the 14th. Following his strict instructions, they had encamped in three areas within a mile or two of the frontier. Thus the improbable had occurred. Blücher and his Prussians on the border, and the English, Dutch, and Belgians, who occupied the country farther west and north, remained scattered. The French campfires had just been spotted. But although Blücher did make some hurried defensive moves, the enemy, overconfident, did not fully grasp what had gone on right under their noses.

Napoleon found his men in high spirits. Many were faithful old soldiers who had been with him on other campaigns.

Napoleon Bonaparte, 1769–1821

There were also young recruits who appeared eager to get into action. Seeing Napoleon in his battle hat and familiar green military coat, the troops broke out in a frenzy which, according to one observer, "bordered on madness."

Addressing the rank and file, Napoleon fanned the flames of their hysteria with the following words: "Soldiers, today is the anniversary of Marengo and of Friedland, occasions which decided the destiny of Europe. . . . We believed in the . . . princes whom we left on their thrones. Today, however, in a coalition against us they grudge the independence and the most sacred rights of France. They have started on the most unjust of aggressions. Let us march, therefore, to encounter them. Are we not the same men as before?

"Soldiers! At Jena, against these same Prussians, today so arrogant, you were one to two, and at Montmirail one to three. Let those among you who have been prisoners of the English tell you the story of their galleys and of the fearful wrongs that they have suffered. . . .

"Soldiers! We shall have to make some forced marches, fight some battles, run some risks; but with constancy, victory will be ours; the rights, the honor, and the happiness of the country will be reconquered.

"For every Frenchman who has courage, the moment has come to conquer or die."

The men cheered until they were hoarse. Then they ate, and, weary from the long march, stretched out on the ground and slept soundly.

But among them, all was not as it seemed. True, their patriotism was at a fever pitch. But behind that, their morale had been weakened by uneasy reservations about their officers. Was it not fickle to switch one's loyalty back and forth between Louis and Napoleon? And would this campaign be both bloody and in the end useless, as Napoleon's others had been? That night a drummer deserted from France's most loyal unit, the Old Guard, to join Blücher's Prussians.

Among the officers there was not only the fear of being charged with treason but the belief that Napoleon had staffed his army poorly, leaving several men best suited for high-command posts in Paris. The same night General Louis Bourmont and his staff deserted to join the enemy.

Thus Napoleon had inspired love and zeal but not con-fidence—the opposite of the situation in Wellington's ranks.

A Wedge

Since daylight comes early to northern France in mid-June, Napoleon directed his troops to move at 2:30 A.M. the next morning for an attack on Charleroi, on the Belgian side. He expected to cross the Sambre River at 9:00 A.M.

A series of misfortunes, however, combined to slow down the attack. A dispatch rider carrying the orders to Van-damme, commander of an important unit of the central force at Beaumont, was thrown from his horse and lay helpless with a broken leg. The orders did not reach Vandamme until almost noon. The responsibility for this lay with an officer at Napoleon's headquarters, who had neglected to send the two messengers usually dispatched in such a case.

Next, Etienne Gérard, commanding the entire right wing at Philippeville, had trouble getting his troops organized and therefore started late. Finally, on orders from Blücher, who had heard about the French forces, the relatively weak Prus-sian border outposts at the gap fought much harder than had been expected, in order to delay the advance and give Blücher time to organize.

It was noon before Napoleon rode up to the Sambre River and ordered the bridges stormed. This was easily accomplished and Charleroi was taken. The Prussians, under J. E. C. Zieten, retreated in haste northeastward to the village of Fleurus. But crucial hours had been lost. Napoleon's failure to appoint the very best men available among his high officers was already beginning to show its effect.

Then, shortly after 3:00 P.M., Marshal Ney arrived hurriedly from Paris. Napoleon had summoned him for a command post at the last minute, somehow having forgotten him before. "The bravest of the brave" were words often applied to Ney, and they suited him well. A man of great courage and inspiration on the battlefield, he could carry out the most difficult tactical assignments with almost unbelievable success. It was in just this way that Napoleon had used him many times before—giving Ney a hard but clear, simple order. Now, however, he turned over command of the entire left flank to Ney, a position calling for very different qualities. Such a post required not bravery but initiative and broad, strategic wisdom—the very attributes Ney lacked. Ney, moreover, knew nothing of the men he was suddenly commanding. By 1815 Ney, already worn, dissipated, and old, had grown erratic and impatient. This appointment would prove Napoleon's greatest mistake of the campaign.

Ney was ordered to "Go and drive the enemy before you on the Brussels road!" But he was to wait short of Quatre Bras for the go-ahead from the Emperor, who envisioned a quick dash to the Belgian capital. Command of the right wing was now given to Emmanuel Grouchy, and it was his task to pursue the Prussians all the way to Fleurus and grind them into the ground.

Napoleon then returned to his headquarters which had

Marshal Ney,
1769–1815

been established at Charleroi. He was satisfied and confident.
He felt that his tactic of speed and surprise had worked in
spite of the initial delay. The wedge had been inserted. He
was confident that the Prussians would be disposed of before
Wellington could come to their aid.

The road to Brussels was straight. The first third of the
distance was clear, about twelve miles to the village of Quatre
Bras, which means "four arms" or "crossroads."

If he encountered no opposition more serious than that
which he had already met, he could reach the outskirts of
the Belgian capital the very next day. If he marched all night,
Saturday morning would see him in Brussels where he
planned to lead his troops through the streets in a victory

parade. He was so confident of success that in his dispatches from Paris he had ordered his soldiers to carry their brilliant red-and-blue dress uniforms in their knapsacks for the triumphal event.

He gave Ney his instructions, then left to join Grouchy in pursuit of Blücher's Prussians.

Wellington's Plans

Napoleon had crossed the Sambre at noon on Thursday the 15th, but it was not until 3:00 P.M. the same day that scanty news of an attack reached Wellington's headquarters in Brussels. Fearing to make a false move, Wellington delayed action, as Napoleon had predicted. He waited for intelligence to arrive from his officers in the field. It was 10 o'clock at night before he issued his first orders.

Then he left for a ball given by the Duchess of Richmond, who, like the wives of many other English officers and men, had come to Brussels with her husband. Why? Did Wellington go to this affair so that suspicions concerning the threatened invasion of the capital should not be aroused? Or because it was also a convenient place for him to confer with his high officers, who were also guests? These explanations have some merit. But there is no doubt that Wellington did not consider the news he had received very threatening. The British were so confident Napoleon would not attack that an officer in the intelligence network had refused to transmit a full report of the attack to Wellington. Not until later in the evening, as more dispatches reached him, did Wellington show any sign of concern. Then, as the dance went gaily on, he whispered to his officers and one by one they slipped away into the night.

The Duke of Wellington, 1769–1852
(Portrait by Sir Thomas Lawrence)

General Blücher, 1742–1819

After the customary midnight supper had been served, Wellington said that it was time for him to go to bed. Rising from the table, he asked his host, privately, if he had a good map in the house. The two men went into the Duke of Richmond's small dressing room, closed the door, and unfolded a map. Wellington pieced together the information that had been filtering in.

"Napoleon has humbugged me, by God!" he exclaimed. "He has gained twenty-four hours' march on me!"

Wellington pointed to Quatre Bras. He had ordered his army to concentrate at points west of there. But if Napoleon could not be stopped at Quatre Bras, he had other plans. "Then I must fight him here," he said, and, with his thumbnail, he traced a line along a ridge bordering certain high ground called Mont-Saint-Jean, just one mile south of the village of Waterloo.

The Crossroads

Wellington was fast asleep at 2:30 in the morning when the richly dressed ladies and their escorts left the Duchess of Richmond's ball. Two hours later with the first blush of dawn, English and other Allied troops began marching through the deserted streets of Brussels, to the sound of drums and shrill pipes. By 8 o'clock that same day, Friday the 16th, Wellington was in the saddle and heading toward the front, passing long columns of his men marching southward toward Quatre Bras.

Arriving at Quatre Bras, Wellington was pleased to find that his Dutch generals garrisoned there had taken the initiative and done the right thing. They had fortified the crossroads formed by the Nivelles-Namur road and the Charleroi-

Brussels road, the "four arms" which gave the town its name. And while their troops were taking their battle positions, he and his staff officers rode eastward along the Nivelles-Namur road to consult with the Prussians.

Wellington found Blücher about seven miles away, occupying a site on a hill topped by a windmill which served as an observation tower. This hill was close to the village of Ligny and only about two miles north of Fleurus, which was now held by the French, the Prussians having been forced to surrender it.

The Duke did not like the exposed position of the Prussian troops on the hill, and he was bold enough to say so. To his criticism, one of the arrogant Prussian staff officers replied that Prussians always liked to see their enemy.

Later, riding back to Quatre Bras, Wellington remarked, "If they fight here, they will be damnably mauled."

Double Threat

While this was going on, Napoleon was standing high in a windmill on the edge of Fleurus, surveying the countryside through a telescope. He could clearly see the Prussian troops encamped on the exposed slope of the hill close to Ligny. He remarked, "The old fox has not gone away."

Napoleon had planned on fighting only one army at a time, but he now realized that he would have to fight on two fronts at once: Ney against Wellington's forces at Quatre Bras, and Grouchy against Blücher's Prussians at Ligny. Yet he was still confident.

News continued to reach him that Wellington's forces were massing at Quatre Bras. Late in the morning, he sent Ney a definite order to attack.

It took four hours for the message to reach Ney. The fighting at Quatre Bras finally began at 2 o'clock in the afternoon. With cheers and the sound of drums and trumpets, the French flung themselves upon the enemy with a frenzy, but the 7,500 Dutch troops holding the village answered with stubborn resistance. Two hours earlier, Ney would have so far outnumbered them that he would have crushed them with ease. But lacking the initiative and strategic mind to do so, he had sat idly by as the enemy forces assembled, while he waited for the precise order to attack.

Since Napoleon was reserving his cavalry for later, Ney's infantry was forced to fight alone, supported only by some artillery. The day was hot and sultry. Their battle squares advanced and engaged the enemy for a full hour in one assault after the other. The acrid odor of gunpowder filled the air. At last the French began to gain the advantage. But then more Allied divisions arrived from Brussels to reinforce the enemy, and Wellington himself took command.

During the next few hours, more and more troops arrived from Brussels to swell Wellington's forces. By late afternoon his force greatly outnumbered the French under Ney. The situation called for cool and careful judgment. But fiery-spirited Ney became desperate, and desperation made him reckless. In one charge he flung away 4,000 men in a futile effort to dislodge Wellington and capture the crossroads!

Wellington, riding a great war horse called Copenhagen, was just the opposite—the model of reason and control. He rode back and forth along his lines, coolly evaluating the changing situation and issuing crisp orders. Several times he was pursued by French cavalry. Once he escaped capture only by swinging his horse about suddenly and jumping across a trench occupied by his Highlanders.

Marshal Ney, in desperation, shouts reckless orders up and down the battle line at Quatre Bras. (Painting by Eugène Chaperon)

Ney Calls for Help

At 5:15 P.M. Ney, unable to force the English line, called urgently for reserves. They consisted of four divisions totaling 20,000 men under the command of Jean Baptiste D'Erlon. But whatever hopes Ney had of receiving help were soon shattered. He learned that D'Erlon, on his own responsibility, had just decided to march his divisions to Ligny to help Grouchy crush Blücher.

Ney was furious. He was about to demand the return of D'Erlon's reserves when he received word from Napoleon, who was still with Grouchy at Fleurus, that he was to seize Quatre Bras unaided and then turn eastward to help crush Blücher. The last line of the order read, "The fate of France is in your hands."

The prospect of continuing without help was more than Ney could face. His rage blinded his reason. He ignored his Emperor's wishes, sending an urgent demand for help to D'Erlon. Not until he received a second dispatch from Napoleon, saying that D'Erlon was needed at Ligny, did he finally accept his fate. Then he plunged once more into the battle.

But during the late afternoon Wellington had received still more fresh troops from Brussels. By 7:00 P.M. he had 33,000 men against Ney's 22,000. Just before darkness fell, he attacked. Over the ground already covered with dead men and horses, he drove the French back to the position they had occupied that morning before the battle started, the town of Fleurus.

Ney's situation was becoming critical. Then the unexpected happened. At 9:00 P.M., as night settled upon the battlefield at Quatre Bras, D'Erlon's reserves began to pour

in. They had marched all the way to the edge of the battlefield at Ligny, received Ney's desperate call, and marched
back to Quatre Bras. Before they could form into battle lines,
however, it was 10:00 P.M., too late to counterattack.

And so the battle of Quatre Bras was still undecided, although during that one day of fighting Wellington lost
4,700 men and the French 4,300.

The Battle of Ligny

The fighting at Ligny had also been fierce and bloody.
At 2:30 P.M., the sound of distant cannons announced that
Ney's attack against Wellington had begun at Quatre Bras.
Napoleon, who had been waiting for that signal, ordered the
assault against Blücher's exposed troops to begin. The men's
spirits were of the highest. The drums beat and the bands
played as they entered the battle.

The Prussians numbered 83,000 to Napoleon's 71,000.
The fight for the villages scattered around Ligny continued
with a cruel relentlessness all through the torrid afternoon.
Village after village was captured and recaptured. The dead
lay in the streets, and the wounded who were able to crawl,
crept into the deserted farmhouses and barns.

At last, the French began to gain an advantage over the
Prussians. Seeing this, Napoleon decided to call in the reserves and force a quick victory. But when at 7:00 P.M. he
suddenly learned that D'Erlon's reserves had headed back
toward Quatre Bras, he realized that Grouchy must defeat
Blücher alone. He was not discouraged. He decided that
Grouchy must not only defeat Blücher at Ligny but deliver
the Prussians such an overwhelming blow that they would
be unfit for further combat.

During the retreat from Ligny, General Blücher is toppled from his favorite horse. (Engraving by Dubourg, after J. A. Atkinson)

Napoleon now called on his faithful Old Guard. These veteran fighters, with their mustaches and great bearskin hats, arrived on the field just in time to counter a last desperate attack by the Prussians. They fought with such courage that the enemy was soon forced to retire. Then, drawing forward their artillery, the Old Guard aimed at the very center of Blücher's exhausted troops. At 7:45 P.M., a salvo from sixty big guns opened fire. The bloody gap blasted by cannon fire proved too much for the Prussians. Their ranks fell apart.

To stem the panic of a disorderly retreat, Blücher himself dashed onto the battlefield. But his fine white charger, a present from the English Regent, was struck by a bullet and fell, pinning him under its full weight. The old marshal was rescued by some of his officers and carried off the field in a hay-filled cart.

By 9:00 P.M. the battle at Ligny was over. The Prussians,

having left their wounded behind, were in full retreat toward the north. But the fast-falling night and the general lack of information concerning Ney at Quatre Bras prevented Grouchy from pursuing them.

D'Erlon's hesitancy in marching back and forth between Quatre Bras and Ligny proved most unfortunate for the French. If his force of 20,000 extra men had come into action at Ligny, then Blücher could have been annihilated. If he had arrived earlier to help Ney at Quatre Bras, then Wellington would have been crushed. But he did neither.

So at Ligny, too, the outcome of the day's fighting fell short of Napoleon's plans. Blücher had been beaten but not destroyed. His Prussians, though badly "mauled," as Wellington had predicted, still remained a threatening force. Here, too, the only definite result was a large death toll.

The fields were covered with the dead and wounded. Blücher lost 12,000 men and Napoleon, 8,500. In and about Ligny, 20,500 men had fallen within an area of only two square miles! These added to the dead at Quatre Bras meant that almost 30,000 men had lost their lives that day.

Despite the inconclusive action at Quatre Bras and the eventual retreat of Blücher, this was the day on which Napoleon really lost the war. By a combination of bad luck and bad judgment, the precious hours leading up to these battles were wasted. Had the first move against Charleroi the day before been made a few hours earlier; had Ney attacked Quatre Bras before so many reinforcements swelled Wellington's ranks; and had Grouchy struck Blücher sooner, the French position on the night of Friday, June 16th, might have been decisive. Better commanders than Ney, Grouchy, or D'Erlon, men who would not have allowed these blunders to occur, were meanwhile idle in Paris.

CHRONOLOGY
I

EVENTS PRECEDING WATERLOO

SATURDAY, JUNE 3, 1815. Blücher writes his wife that Bonaparte will never dare attack. On the contrary, he says the Allied invasion of France will soon begin.

TUESDAY, JUNE 6. The French armies move out. National Guardsmen move into the former camps so the absence of the army troops will not be noticed.

WEDNESDAY, JUNE 7. A close watch is clamped down along the entire Belgian frontier to prevent any news getting through. All coastal traffic is stopped. False information is carefully leaked out to the enemy. To make Wellington think he has decided to cut off the British lines of supply at the seacoast, Bonaparte spreads rumors of troop movements toward Lille and Dunkerque.

SUNDAY, JUNE 11, JUST BEFORE MIDNIGHT. Napoleon slips secretly out of Paris. His carriage rushes toward the Belgian border at breakneck speed. The trip takes nearly three days, during which time Napoleon's troops quietly establish camps within a mile or two of the frontier.

TUESDAY, JUNE 13. A Prussian outpost at Charleroi spots campfires on the French side of the border. Large encampments at Beaumont and Solre are discovered. A courier is dispatched to find Blücher and give him the alarming news. But he is at Namur, a border town some thirty miles northeast of Charleroi.

Wellington, comfortably established in Brussels, writes to a friend that the Allied forces in Belgium are too strong for Napoleon even to think of attacking.

WEDNESDAY, JUNE 14. Word of the French troops reaches Blücher. He dispatches an order for his forces to mass at Sombreffe, ten miles back from the border, and directs smaller units to delay the French if they invade. But he forgets to have the bridges over the Sambre destroyed.

WEDNESDAY, JUNE 14, EVENING. Napoleon arrives to take command of his troops. His plan is working perfectly. There are 124,000 French troops massed along the frontier, ready for an assault. Across the Sambre River, the border, Wellington's and Blücher's forces are scattered as widely as ever. No effort has been made to close the gap. The impossible has been accomplished. Napoleon gives a rousing speech to his men.

WEDNESDAY, JUNE 14, LATE. Two men desert, showing that, despite apparent high spirits, morale is not at its best. One, a drummer, leaves from France's toughest and most faithful unit, the Old Guard. General Bourmont, who took his staff to join Louis XVIII and the Allies, is the other.

To take full advantage of the element of surprise, Napoleon decides to attack at once. After crossing the Sambre, his right-wing unit will push toward Blücher; the left, toward Wellington. The central mass of reserves will then be free to join whichever wing encountered a main force of the enemy first. His orders state the army will move at 2:30 A.M.

THURSDAY, JUNE 15, MORNING. Napoleon suffers unexpected delays:

1. A dispatch rider carrying the order to Vandamme, commander of an important unit of the central force, is thrown from his horse and is lying helpless with a broken leg. Vandamme does not receive his orders until almost noon.

2. Because of difficulties in organizing his troops, Gérard, commanding the entire right wing at Philippeville, starts late.

3. Napoleon has anticipated crossing the Charleroi bridge by 9 A.M. But because the Prussian outposts fight much harder than was expected, it is not crossed until noon.

1:00 P.M. In Brussels, Wellington still knows nothing of what is going on. He writes a letter to a division commander suggesting, for reasons of British tradition, a renumbering of the divisions. And he writes to the Czar of Russia, saying that he expects to invade France the end of June. Pleasantly, Wellington looks forward to a ball he is to attend that evening.

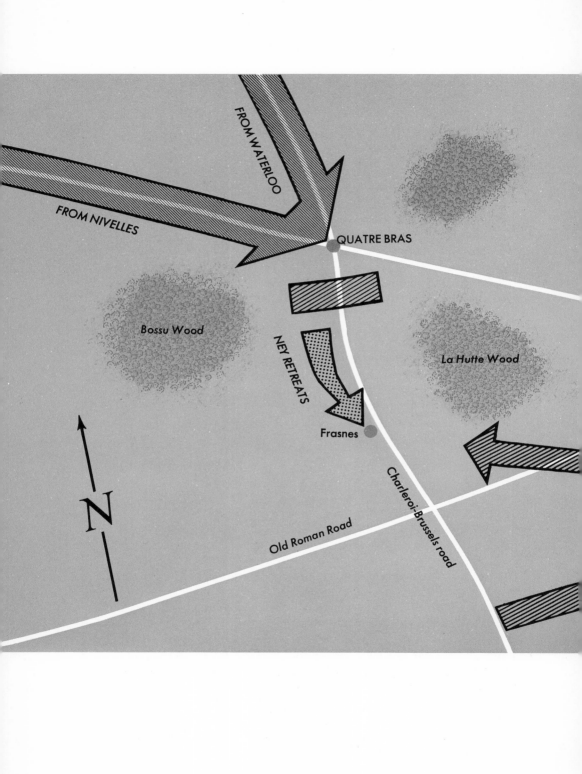

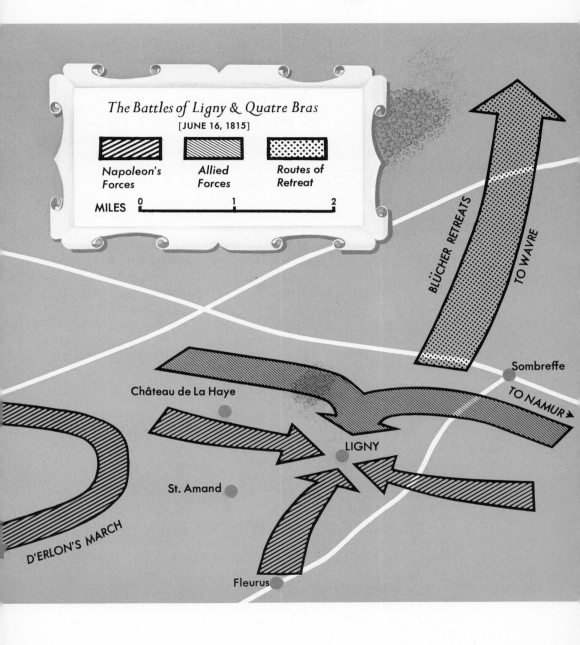

The Battles of Ligny & Quatre Bras

[JUNE 16, 1815]

Napoleon's Forces   Allied Forces   Routes of Retreat

MILES   0   1   2

BLÜCHER RETREATS

TO WAVRE

Sombreffe

TO NAMUR

Château de La Haye

LIGNY

St. Amand

D'ERLON'S MARCH

Fleurus

3:00 P.M.   The first news reaches Wellington. But it says only that gunfire was heard about 4:30 that morning. Owing to a serious breakdown in the British intelligence network, many hours are to go by before he receives more definite word. Just as Napoleon has predicted, Wellington waits for the facts to come in before making any decision.

3:15 P.M.   Marshal Ney arrives to join the French Army. Napoleon, badly in need of a commander for his left wing, gives him the post. Ney and the left wing are to wait on the road beyond Charleroi. When they receive the go-ahead from the Emperor, they are to "Go and drive the enemy before you on the Brussels road!" For various reasons Ney is ill-suited to this job, and Napoleon's hasty and perhaps sentimental assignment will prove the most serious mistake of the campaign.

5:30 P.M.   Napoleon, anxious to know how his right flank is progressing, goes to the front. He discovers that Grouchy, the commander, and Vandamme, who has finally arrived to lend assistance against the Prussians, have been debating how to proceed for two hours. Typically, Napoleon does not debate, but acts. The right wing plunges ahead, and the Prussians retreat. As darkness falls, the French halt for the night at Fleurus.

10:00 P.M.   Wellington finally receives positive word that the French are attacking, and issues his first definitive order. He instructs bodies of his troops to concentrate at points west of Quatre Bras, a town on the Charleroi-Brussels road (in the path of Ney's drive). Then, still poorly informed, Wellington leaves for the ball.

JUST BEFORE MIDNIGHT.   Dispatches reach Wellington at intervals. He stays at the ball, showing no apparent concern, although he whispers occasionally with his officers, who one by one slip away.

DAWN.   Wellington and troops from Brussels move southward down the road toward Quatre Bras. Other Allied units approach Quatre Bras from the west.

6 A.M.   Napoleon, at Charleroi, has lain prostrate on his bed with fatigue, unable to function during the precious wee hours of the morning—a serious loss. Since no British troops have been reported, Napoleon mistakenly concludes that Wellington's forces are falling back to concentrate on Brussels.

8 A.M.   Napoleon finally orders Grouchy's right wing to move forward again against the Prussians and to push them from Fleurus, to Ligny, to Sombreffe, and if possible as far as Gembloux.

8:30 A.M.   Napoleon sends Ney his first dispatch of the day, informing him of Grouchy's orders. Ney is to occupy Quatre Bras, which is to be a simple matter, to prevent any of Wellington's troops from coming across to join Blücher. Then, when the right wing has captured Gembloux, Ney is to dash to Brussels and be there by the evening of the next day.

9:00 A.M.   Blücher, having decided to fight at Ligny, masses his troops there.

9:30 A.M.   Wellington reaches his troops at Quatre Bras.

10:00 A.M.   Napoleon receives news of mounting Allied forces at Quatre Bras. He immediately sends a second dispatch to Ney, ordering him to push forward at once. Then the Emperor rides off to join Grouchy.

11:00 A.M.   Napoleon's first, somewhat vague orders reach Ney. Seeing the forces mounting in front of him, Ney should have taken the initiative long before this, even, and crushed them. But Ney has waited for an exact order.

NOON.   Wellington, realizing that his greatest strength lies in unity with the Prussians, and believing all will remain quiet at Quatre Bras, rides to find Blücher and work out a co-ordinated battle strategy with him.

2:00 P.M.   Napoleon's second orders, to attack immediately, finally reach Ney. Although Ney could have taken Quatre Bras easily a few hours before, the enemy now is much stronger, as Wellington's units have continued to arrive.

Ney attacks. The fighting is rough, but slowly the French gain the advantage.

2:30 P.M.   Napoleon, with Grouchy on the right wing, hears the sound of Ney's cannons and orders the assault against Blücher.

3:00 P.M.   New units arrive to swell the British forces at Quatre Bras, evening the odds there.

3:15 P.M.   The battle on the right flank rages fiercely around Ligny. Napoleon, still unaware that Ney is having a difficult time, orders him to take Quatre Bras quickly, then move eastward to help crush Blücher.

5:00 P.M.   Many more British troops have poured into Quatre Bras. Ney is now badly outnumbered. Irritable, desperate, and still without the kind of orders he needs to function well, he begins to give reckless commands. He badly needs the central reserve force under D'Erlon.

5:15 P.M. Ney calls desperately for D'Erlon's reserves, then learns that D'Erlon has taken it on himself to march the other way, toward Ligny. Ney is furious. Just then Napoleon's instructions arrive, to capture Quatre Bras quickly, then come to help fight Blücher. The last line reads, "The fate of France is in your hands." Ney flies into a rage. He sends another urgent request to D'Erlon. A third dispatch comes from Napoleon, saying that D'Erlon is needed at Ligny.

6:00 P.M. D'Erlon, with 30,000 troops, comes to the outskirts of Napoleon's right-flank force. At that moment Ney's desperate message reaches him. D'Erlon thereupon turns around and heads toward Quatre Bras.

7:15 P.M. Wellington, his forces swollen still larger, attacks Ney along the whole Quatre Bras front, driving the French back.

7:45 P.M. Napoleon, without D'Erlon, launches a tremendous assault which smashes the Prussian center. Blücher is wounded. The French push forward.

9:00 P.M. The battles on both fronts are halted by darkness. The Prussians are in full retreat, pulling northward toward Brussels. Blücher sends an aide-de-camp to warn Wellington what has happened, but the messenger is shot. Wellington remains hazy about the results at Ligny.

D'Erlon's reserves reach Ney, too late. Ney has been pushed back to Frasnes. The reserves, badly needed on both fronts, have not fired a shot all day.

SATURDAY, JUNE 17, 10:00 A.M. Wellington opens his withdrawal from Quatre Bras.

NOON. The last of the British forces are evacuated.

2:00 P.M. Napoleon reaches Quatre Bras and is shocked to learn that Ney has allowed Wellington to retreat in plain view. He exclaims to D'Erlon: "France has been lost! Come on, my dear general, put yourself at the head of the cavalry and close on the English rear guard!" The French pursue but are delayed by a thunderstorm.

6:30 P.M. The French halt at and around La Belle Alliance, a tavern. Unable to see Wellington's positions in the misty, fading light, Napoleon skillfully induces Wellington to give away his position by firing toward him and noting the replies. But by now it is too late to attack, and Napoleon exclaims, "Would to God I had Joshua's power to stop the sun for two hours!"

Blücher Retreats

The next day, Saturday, June 17th, was the day on which Napoleon had planned to lead his victorious troops through the streets of Brussels. Instead, he was checkmated in the field where he was preparing to engage the enemy once more. So, with the coming of light, he began to reorganize his fighting forces.

At this same early hour, Wellington was also re-examining his position. He did not know that Blücher had been defeated at Ligny the night before, because the officer bringing the news had been shot. Therefore, early in the morning Wellington sent a group of cavalry officers to establish contact with his ally, the Prussians. The officers returned at 7:30 A.M. with the shocking report that Blücher was in full retreat toward the village of Wavre, about thirteen miles north of Ligny and only fifteen miles from Brussels.

Wellington found this news hard to believe. In fact, it was not until 9:00 P.M., when an officer from Blücher's headquarters confirmed the report, that he was finally convinced.

The British commander then made his plans. In order to keep the Allied forces close to each other—the very thing Napoleon feared—he decided to withdraw to the north, across wheat fields and woods, to a position only ten miles away from Wavre. He sent Blücher a dispatch saying that he was falling back to the high ground and ridge south of Waterloo known as Mont-Saint-Jean, and that he would engage Napoleon at that point if Blücher would support him.

Blücher had been carried almost unconscious from the battlefield at Ligny, but he was not seriously hurt. There were no broken bones; he was only badly shaken up and bruised. With the aid of a brew of "gin and rhubarb," he

Napoleon's "Old Grumblers," the Old Guard, on the battlefield

was soon well enough to rejoin his staff. And so, although the 73-year-old marshal had spent a very uncomfortable night, and although his troops were still retreating, he was willing to act in accord with Wellington's plan.

Precious Hours Again Lost

Napoleon should have taken advantage of Blücher's retreat and moved troops from the right flank to Quatre Bras to attack Wellington again on the morning of the 17th, before the Iron Duke had a chance to withdraw to the ridge south of Waterloo.

But Napoleon was exhausted and needed time to recast his plans. He had left Paris shortly after midnight on the 12th and had been subjected to tremendous strain day and night for the next five days, or until 11 o'clock the night of Friday the 16th, when he returned from the bloody field at Ligny.

He was no longer as energetic and alert as he had been in the past. His year of exile at Elba had brought about many physical changes. He had grown heavy, almost fat. Sitting on a horse pained him. He tired easily and dozed off at unexpected moments.

He needed rest and he needed time, as his dispatch to his officers issued at 8:00 A.M. reveals, "to terminate this operation, to supply ammunition, bring in stragglers, and call detachments. . . ." Therefore, he could not press his advantage over Blücher.

Besides, he had not yet heard from Ney. The marshal delayed his report, both because it was not a happy one, and because he was angry with the Emperor. He blamed Napoleon for having called the reserves to Ligny when their presence at Quatre Bras would have given him victory over Wellington before nightfall.

Grouchy's Delay

Napoleon thus spent the precious early morning of the 17th resting and planning instead of attacking the enemy. Suspecting that Ney had not properly used all the forces at his disposal, he ordered him to send a complete report on the exact deployment of all his divisions. As for the Prussians, he ordered Grouchy to "pursue" them and find out exactly what they intended to do. Having heard a rumor that some Prussians were moving eastward toward Liége and the German border, he asked hopefully, "Are they separating themselves from the English?"

Napoleon assumed that Grouchy would set out immediately in pursuit of the enemy as ordered, but this was not the case. Grouchy felt that his men needed a full morning of rest. They needed time to eat their bread and soup and time to clean their guns. Since the Prussians were retreating anyway, he thought there was no need for haste.

It was therefore 2:00 P.M. before Grouchy's troops got started. And no sooner did they begin marching than a sudden downpour turned the roads into mud, making them almost impassable. The horses could barely drag the artillery. Grouchy's 33,000 men were able to cover only eight miles before night closed in.

Wellington Withdraws

After giving his orders to Grouchy, Napoleon had decided to lead a force of men to Quatre Bras to reinforce Ney. He himself would deal Wellington the decisive blow. From Quatre Bras to Brussels was twenty miles: he would be there the next day.

But while Napoleon marched to join Ney, Wellington, wisely subordinating everything to the main goal of uniting with Blücher, was conducting a well-planned withdrawal from Quatre Bras in broad daylight and within sight of Ney's whole French Army. It was a delicate operation, but it went off without a hitch. The Duke, strict and exacting, remained behind until the last with a rear guard of cavalry and cannons, to make sure that everything was carried out correctly. He watched the French through his long telescope and now and then ordered his cannons to fire, just to make his presence known and to prove he was unafraid. Nevertheless, when his last company finally marched off, the Duke said, "Well, there is the last of the infantry gone, and I don't care now."

Dark storm clouds which had been gathering, now broke.

Wellington marches confidently from Quatre Bras to Waterloo, the scene of Napoleon's final defeat. (Painting by E. Crofts)

There were thunder and lightning. Heavy rains drenched the green wheat fields that stretched as far as the eye could see. And in the midst of it all, Napoleon arrived, riding his favorite white mare. His greatcoat was drenched; the brim of his famous battle hat had collapsed. Through the sheets of rain he saw Wellington's retreating rear guard. Recognizing them, he cried out: "Fire! They are the English!"

His men obeyed. They fired, but Wellington's troops continued their orderly withdrawal and were soon lost in the misty distance. Still another critical loss of time and position had occurred. For the second day in a row, Ney had failed to take the initiative and attack. Had he done so, his forces, swelled by D'Erlon's, could have crushed Wellington. Now Wellington was on his way north, where he intended to unite with Blücher, the very thing Napoleon's plan had been designed to prevent.

Through the driving rain and across muddy fields, the

French plodded after the British. They sank down to their
knees in the mire, and many lost their boots. About a mile
from the ridge south of Waterloo, at a wayside inn called
La Belle Alliance, Napoleon called a halt.

The rain had stopped. As the mist lifted, the Emperor
rode out to see if he could locate the British and Dutch forces.
He suspected that they had taken their position on Mont-
Saint-Jean astride the Brussels road just a mile and a half
away, but he was not certain. He ordered a few rounds to
be fired in that direction by his advance artillery. The cannons boomed; promptly, there came a sharp reply.

Now he knew. Wellington was waiting. Blücher was
dangerously near, but Napoleon, still confident, decided that
in the morning he would blow the "obstruction" apart and
march on to Brussels.

He rode back along the Brussels-Charleroi road and established his headquarters in a little farmhouse, the Caillou
house, about a mile and a half south of La Belle Alliance. As
he dried out before a roaring fire, he stared through a window
at his troops trudging past. They were blue with cold, and
hunched over under knapsacks which weighed as much as
sixty-five pounds.

Once more it rained, this time without mercy. The thousands of men who made up Napoleon's army, their morale
already shaken, were forced to spend the night in the water-
soaked fields. Somehow, they managed to build campfires.
Around these fires they huddled, eating large hunks of bread
and bowls of watery soup made from scraps the local peasants
gave them. Their provision wagons, bogged down in the
mud, had been left far behind. And then, weary to the point
of exhaustion, they rolled up in their blankets on the sodden
ground and slept.

A Midnight Ride . . .

Wellington spent the early hours of that same rainy night (June 17th) in a house in Waterloo writing dispatches. Then toward midnight he ordered his charger Copenhagen to be saddled, and with only one trusted orderly he set out on the road to Wavre. He wanted to learn from Blücher's own lips the exact hour when their forces would join. After all, the French had 260 cannons to his 156. He needed the weight of Blücher's forces.

Wellington knew that one branch of Blücher's retreating army was now camped at Wavre about twelve miles away. But he did not find "Old Forwards," as he called him, until he traveled two miles farther in the rain. "However," said Wellington, "I saw him and got the information from him."

The night was so dark that on the way back Copenhagen and the Iron Duke fell into a ditch. But the orderly helped pull them out, so they got back safely to Waterloo.

. . . and a Midnight Walk

At 1:00 A.M. it was still raining when Napoleon, rising from his cot, walked out into the night. Looking across the blackness toward the distant ridge, he could see the glow of the enemy's fires. Wellington was still there.

Satisfied, Napoleon returned to the farmhouse. There he found a dispatch from Grouchy stating that the main Prussian force was heading for Liége, just as he had hoped. A smaller force, however, appeared to be falling back to Wavre. Napoleon, believing Grouchy was taking immediate steps to head off these Prussians and prevent their joining with Wellington, was pleased.

Napoleon on the eve of June 18, 1815 (Painting by Charlet)

PART THREE

THE FATAL DAY

Battle Positions

It rained all night long. But in spite of this, Napoleon's men were called shortly after midnight. They were marched forward to take their battle positions only 1,300 yards from Wellington's ridge. The rain did not let up until 6:00 A.M., the time Napoleon had set for the battle to start. But the mists were very heavy and the ground drenched, with pools in every hollow; therefore the battle could not begin at once.

At about 7:30 A.M., Napoleon received a report from some of his outposts that Wellington's forces were retiring. Could such a thing be possible? Would Wellington deprive him of victory this day? The Emperor, accompanied by some of his staff, rode out to the front to check for himself. Reaching an advanced position, he saw the enemy through the mist and drizzle. But he wanted to be certain. He dismounted and walked still closer to the enemy line. Now he could clearly see that the enemy was not retreating. Instead, Wellington was busy reinforcing his battle positions.

From where Napoleon stood, the soggy wheat fields sloped

A view of La Belle Alliance painted on a plate. The full porcelain service was a gift to Wellington from the King of Prussia.

gently downward for about a quarter of a mile. Then they rose gently for another quarter of a mile to the ridge where, against the misty sky, he could see enemy cannons mounted.

To the right, in the midst of the wheat fields, Napoleon saw the buildings of a farm known as La Haye Sainte, which was situated on the Charleroi-Brussels road. It was heavily fortified by Wellington's forces. To the left he could see the outbuildings, garden wall, hedges, and small grove which clustered about a large, old building known as the Château Hougoumont. This place was also occupied by the enemy.

Napoleon was pleased that Wellington had not escaped him. He spoke to those of his staff who were standing nearby: "Order the men to make their soup, to get their pieces in order, and we will determine what is to be done before noon."

Returning to headquarters, Napoleon ate breakfast. Then he spread out his maps and announced to the officers present that their chances this time were good. How good? He replied that they had ninety chances out of a hundred in their favor. "He has thrown the dice, and they are for us," he said confidently.

One of the officers suggested that Napoleon send for Grouchy's troops. Here were 33,000 men.

But the Emperor brushed this idea aside, saying, "Wellington is a bad general, the English are bad troops, and it will be a picnic." Napoleon assumed Grouchy would block Blücher from joining Wellington, brushing aside a report that Blücher was close to Wavre.

Still confident of victory, later that morning, as the ground drained and the mist began to clear, Napoleon remarked, "If they carry out my orders properly, we will sleep in Brussels tonight." In his pocket he had a proclamation to the citizens of Brussels saying that he, Napoleon, Emperor of France, had heard their plea and had come to make them Frenchmen once more.

The Iron Duke and the Emperor

The two armies facing each other on the field at Waterloo were numerically almost equal. Wellington had 67,000 men of which about 30,000 were British. Of his 156 cannons, 78 were British. Napoleon had 72,000 men, all French, and 246 cannons.

Napoleon had drawn up his army in three lines, in full view of the enemy. The first line, made up mostly of infantry, was to launch the attack. The second line, made up mostly of cavalry, was to back up the first line. The third line, made up of the Guard, Old and Young, infantry and cavalry, all in bearskin hats, would come in for the kill.

Wellington enjoyed a much stronger position. His troops and artillery were entrenched on the ridge in a line running

Napoleon and his officers survey the half-mile of sodden ground that separates the Allies and the French near Mont-Saint-Jean.

from east to west for approximately three miles. Behind this line, in a shallow valley, hidden from Napoleon's view, his reserves were encamped.

Wellington's advantage was counterbalanced, however, by Napoleon's superior artillery and cavalry. And while British morale was equal to that of the French, the same cannot be said of the Dutch, Belgian, and North German troops under Wellington. The Duke tried to offset this shortcoming by carefully intermingling his troops. The halfhearted and inexperienced, of which he had so many, were supported and influenced by those who were "better disciplined and more accustomed to war."

Napoleon ordered the cannons moved into position by 9:30 A.M. Seventy-eight cannons, many of them 12-pounders, were brought to the right side of the Charleroi-Brussels road where D'Erlon's division had been placed, only six hundred yards from the enemy. This was the reserve force that had marched back and forth between Quatre Bras and Ligny two days before without fighting. Now they were in the front line of attack. They were not, however, the first of Napoleon's troops to go into action.

Château Hougoumont

At 11:30 A.M., June 18th, as the men cheered and the drums beat and the bands played "Let Us Watch over the Empire," Napoleon ordered the battle to begin. The first action, an attack by his left flank on Château Hougoumont, was intended only as a diversion. The main attack was to take place on the right and would employ D'Erlon's forces.

The salvo that opened the battle at 11:30 on this Sunday morning, filling the misty air with a heavy cloud of smoke, was heard for miles around. Even Grouchy and his officers, thirteen miles away, heard the rumble of the cannons. They, too, had been waiting all morning for the mist to rise and the roads to dry, before setting out again in pursuit of the fleeing Prussians.

Some of Grouchy's officers suggested that he change his plans and move his troops toward the sound of the guns instead of pursuing the Prussians farther. But Grouchy did not like to change plans nor did he welcome advice. He claimed he had clear orders to continue to pursue the Prussians.

This, however, was not the case. Napoleon's orders were vague, as they so often were during this entire campaign. And the fact that Grouchy had lost contact with Blücher changed the situation completely. It also should have been evident to Grouchy that, by pursuing Blücher now, he could only drive the Prussians *toward* the English on Mont-Saint-Jean, and could no longer hope to perform the function of a wedge.

The attack on Château Hougoumont, with about 8,000 men from the left division, was under the command of Prince Jerome, one of Napoleon's brothers. It proved a very costly affair. The château, with its garden walls and stone buildings, was like a fortress. While the French infantry fought with boiling courage, the men paid heavily for every inch of ground.

Jerome's men succeeded in taking the orchard and grove, but from behind the garden walls and windows of the house they were picked off, one by one, by Wellington's muskets. Indeed, the enemy resistance was so successful that two French forces had to come to Jerome's assistance.

In the end, Château Hougoumont remained in the hands of the British Guards who occupied it, and a ring of dead French soldiers encircled it, their red-and-blue uniforms caked with the mud in which they lay. And so the attack proved to be an inexcusable waste of human lives and military resources on the part of the French High Command. Unfortunately it set the pattern for many other encounters in Waterloo. During that long afternoon, while the fate of Europe hung in the balance, the desperation and recklessness first displayed at Hougoumont were to be repeated at least a hundred times.

Wellington's Ridge

The main operation of the day, on Napoleon's right flank, now began.

The seventy-eight cannons placed in front of D'Erlon's division, only six hundred yards from the enemy, opened fire promptly at 12 o'clock. They were to soften up the enemy

The fierce attack on Château Hougoumont, led by Prince Jerome, one of Napoleon's brothers, was meant to be only a diversionary action, but it cost many French lives even before the day's main operation was begun. (Engraving by Sutherland)

position around the farm, La Haye Sainte. The pounding continued for a full hour and a half. And when its thundering murder stopped, the signal was given for the first charge of the day. Precisely at 1:30 P.M., Napoleon gave Ney the signal. Under cover of heavy cannon smoke which still hung low, D'Erlon's charge began, a charge intended to break through Wellington's center and open the road to Brussels.

The bombardment had been concentrated on Wellington's Dutch-Belgian divisions. After being exposed to the fury of fire from seventy-eight big cannons for well over an hour, the men's spirits were completely shattered. They were not able to stand up to the charge of French infantry coming swiftly across the wheat fields. They broke ranks and threw away their arms in wild confusion. Pushing and sliding on the slippery ground, they rushed back up the slope to the safety of Wellington's line on the crest, with the French close behind them.

A large number of D'Erlon's men were now at the crest of Wellington's ridge. But they were not destined to hold this position, because once more a blunder had been made by the French High Command. The men were organized in long unwieldy columns, the worst possible formation. As a result, when they tried to press over the crest of the ridge, they received the full fire of British infantry at short range.

Then, still staggering from the British fire, and attempting

The British heavy cavalry sweeps through the French ranks, dealing D'Erlon's men a devastating blow which weakens Napoleon's already weary main force. (Painting by R. Simkin)

to spread out their dense ranks and thus correct the error of their ill-suited formation, the French were met by a charge of heavy British cavalry. Riding upon powerful horses and carrying long sabers, the British assaulted the French columns with murderous fury. They cut through the densely massed French troops, bringing confusion, mutilation, and death. The trampled wheat was stained with blood; over the din of the battle could be heard the cries and groans of the wounded and dying.

Two French Eagles were captured by the British; many prisoners were taken; fifteen cannons were disabled; and three columns were turned back in disorder. When the British cavalry returned to the base of the ridge, Wellington was awaiting them, sitting astride Copenhagen. Ordinarily very reserved toward his fighting men, he was so pleased that he received them with a slight lift of his low cocked hat and the words, "Life Guards! I thank you."

The Prussians Return

Napoleon witnessed this disaster with dismay. A series of small setbacks—a blunder here, a bit of bad luck there—had delayed his march on Brussels. Now, as he looked through his spyglass, he spotted something even more ominous.

Four miles away to the east, on some heights called Saint Lambert, he saw a dark mass moving toward his right flank. Some of his officers insisted that it was only the shadow of a passing cloud. But no: the Prussians were coming!

Napoleon at once sent a dispatch to Grouchy saying, "A battle is in progress on the line of Waterloo—the Prussians are approaching." Grouchy and his forces were, therefore, to come to the rescue immediately.

But once more the delivery of a dispatch was delayed. This time the rider did not break a leg nor was he shot. He was simply unable to find Marshal Grouchy, who, wandering about trying to locate the Prussians, had lost all contact with his headquarters. Napoleon's message, therefore, only reached Grouchy between 6 and 7 o'clock that evening. It was now too late to bring his 33,000 men to Napoleon's aid.

Keenly aware of the serious threat on his right, Napoleon ordered Ney to attack La Haye Sainte, the farmhouse on the Brussels road directly in front of Wellington's center. Here again the assault was reckless and expensive. The battle for this single farmhouse began soon after 3:00 P.M. and lasted all afternoon. Ney used the bravest French officers and men, where a few heavy guns could have blasted out the defenders.

Under heavy cannon fire, Wellington's Anglo-Dutch forces withdrew up the hill. Here, within the safety of Wellington's line on the reverse slope of the ridge, they hoped to escape the full force of the French cannonading.

Mistaking this tactical withdrawal for a retreat, Ney decided the time had come for him to attack Wellington's main line of defense. To this end he drew up forty-three squadrons and several thousand men and horses on the hillside in front of La Belle Alliance, forming a line over a half a mile in length. Ney drew his saber, placed himself at the head of the line, and led the charge.

Mounted upon great horses, with their sabers held high, banners flying and bugles blowing, with shouts of "Vive l'Empereur!" the French cavalry galloped down the sloping fields. Past La Haye Sainte and up the hill toward Wellington's line, they rushed forward with terrific force, the hoofs of their horses pounding the ground. Cannon balls whistled overhead. But this did not deter them. They rode at full speed through the heavy battle smoke which hung close to the ground and over the huddled bodies of their comrades who had already fallen.

The result of the charge was gruesome, but Ney would not accept defeat. He now called thirty-seven fresh squadrons onto the field. And he rallied those just hurled backward to attack again.

Once more the line was formed. Once more the men charged forward, shouting "Vive l'Empereur!" The results were no better. Again the French cavalry became hopelessly entangled between the solid squares of British infantry. In desperation they hurled their lances like javelins into the enemy. But even this was of no avail. Lacking the support of their own infantry, the French horsemen were finally routed.

The serious situation at La Haye Sainte was made more desperate by the sudden arrival on the battlefield of the Prussians, 31,000 strong. Just when the fighting was at its worst, these Prussians under Friedrich Wilhelm von Bülow suddenly attacked the French right flank. Napoleon immediately had to deploy some troops which he desperately needed at La Haye Sainte to fight them off. In the end, these forces were pushed back into a section to the east known as Paris Wood. But how long could they be held there? And how soon would the rest of Blücher's troops arrive?

With the Prussian threat temporarily reduced, however, Napoleon once more ordered Ney to capture La Haye Sainte —and to take it at any cost.

Leading the wreckage of D'Erlon's reserves, Ney attacked at once. Again the fighting was hard and bloody. But then at last, at 6:00 P.M., he fulfilled the Emperor's wishes by capturing the little farm.

← TO BRUSSELS

Forest of Soignies

WATERLOO

Mont-Saint-Jean

Braine-l'Alleud

La Haye Sainte

Château Hougoumont

Mon Plaisir

Haine River

⤶⤷ *The Battle of Waterloo* ⤶⤷
[NOON, JUNE 18]

Napoleon	*Wellington*	*Blücher*	*Bülow*

INFANTRY	ARTILLERY	CAVALRY

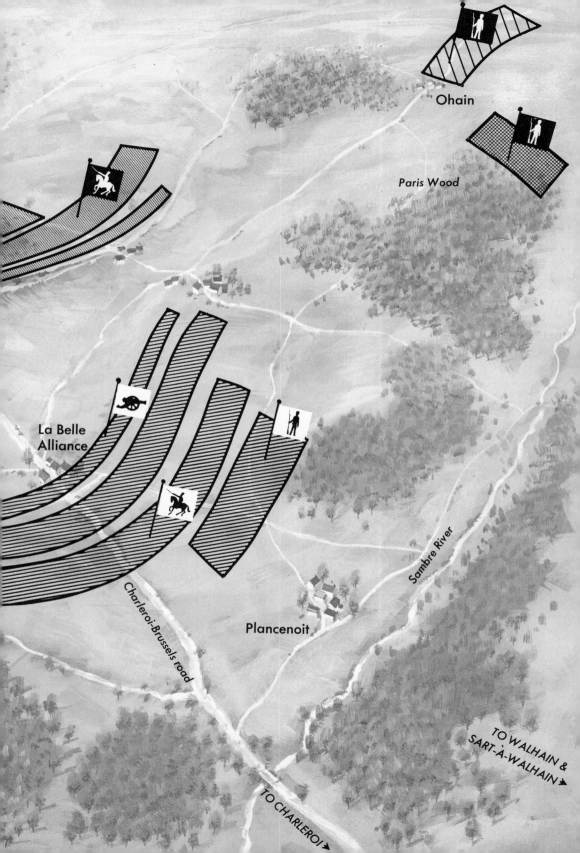

Ohain

Paris Wood

La Belle
Alliance

Sambre River

Plancenoit

Charleroi-Brussels road

TO WALHAIN &
SART-À-WALHAIN ▸

TO CHARLEROI ▸

CHRONOLOGY
II

THE BATTLE—HOUR BY HOUR

SUNDAY, JUNE 18, 1:00 A.M. Napoleon rides out to the front to observe Wellington's positions. He is out at least two hours.

2:00 A.M. A dispatch from Grouchy arrives at La Belle Alliance, written at 10:00 P.M., the 17th. Grouchy says he is unsure which way Blücher is moving. If Blücher heads for Wavre, which lies in the direction of both Brussels and Waterloo, Grouchy plans to follow the Prussians "in order that they might not be able to gain Brussels, and to separate them from Wellington." Grouchy is not thinking clearly. Blücher is moving toward Waterloo, not Brussels. It is impossible for Grouchy to head him off. Grouchy can prevent a meeting of Blücher and Wellington at Waterloo only by marching immediately to join Napoleon. However, he does not know that the battle is coming at Waterloo.

Grouchy's messenger waits for an answer, but none is sent. Clearly Napoleon must tell him what he knows of Blücher's position, the uselessness of trying to pursue Blücher from the rear, and the forthcoming battle at Waterloo.

This is a crucial oversight. Grouchy is left with poor intelligence and no orders. It may be that Napoleon does not know of Grouchy's note, since he is still reconnoitering.

3:30 A.M. Inexplicably, Grouchy delays further and starts in the other direction from Waterloo—to Sart-à-Walhain.

7:30 A.M. The rain has stopped. Napoleon receives a report that Wellington is pulling back, and rides again to the front to see for himself. He finds Wellington is not retiring. But in view of the muddy ground, he puts off the attack, originally scheduled for between 8:00 and 9:00 A.M., to 1:00 P.M.

9:00 A.M.   The entire French Army is marshaled in a grand display, forming ranks in a series of *W*'s in full view of the Allied forces. The bands play; the men shout "Vive l'Empereur!"

Wellington, never having seen such display before, is impressed. But he places his army carefully and calmly awaits the attack. His engineers have studied the whole battlefield carefully and mapped it precisely. Wellington, on the higher ground, knows he has the superior position. His troops are deployed particularly well to withstand the French artillery, which he knows to be fierce. He has arrayed them on the reverse slope of the hill of Mont-Saint-Jean. Also, the slippery ground favors the defense, for it impedes movement. Finally, every moment that the attack is delayed is in his favor, for Blücher is on the way.

10:00 A.M.   The first order of the day to Grouchy is dispatched from the French Command. Written by General Soult, and not revised by Napoleon, it vaguely instructs Grouchy to move toward Wavre.

At almost the same moment, Grouchy arrives at Sart-à-Walhain and sits down to a leisurely breakfast. His dispatch to Napoleon reflects his utter confusion. Blücher is heading for Brussels on the Charleroi-Brussels road, he says, and he himself expects to move between Wellington and Blücher at Wavre. Elementary geography proves this impossible. At the end of his note, Grouchy says that he assumes Wellington is retreating before the French advance.

11:00 A.M.   Grouchy has moved from Sart-à-Walhain to Walhain when he hears the sound of Napoleon's opening cannon fire clearly. His officers urge him to move immediately to join Napoleon. But at this crucial moment personal feelings seem to influence Grouchy against accepting this advice. Grouchy's son, who is with him, writes that "Grouchy did not find the advice bad in itself, but the form employed to present it." He claims—falsely—that he had formal orders to stay in pursuit of the Prussians.

11:30 A.M.   Napoleon opens the battle with an assault on the Château Hougoumont intended to divert Wellington. His brother, Jerome, commands the attack and beats the English on the fields surrounding the fortress. Lieutenant Legros, "an officer of vast strength," smashes the gate of the château with an ax and enters with his men. But Legros and his men are slaughtered and the gate is

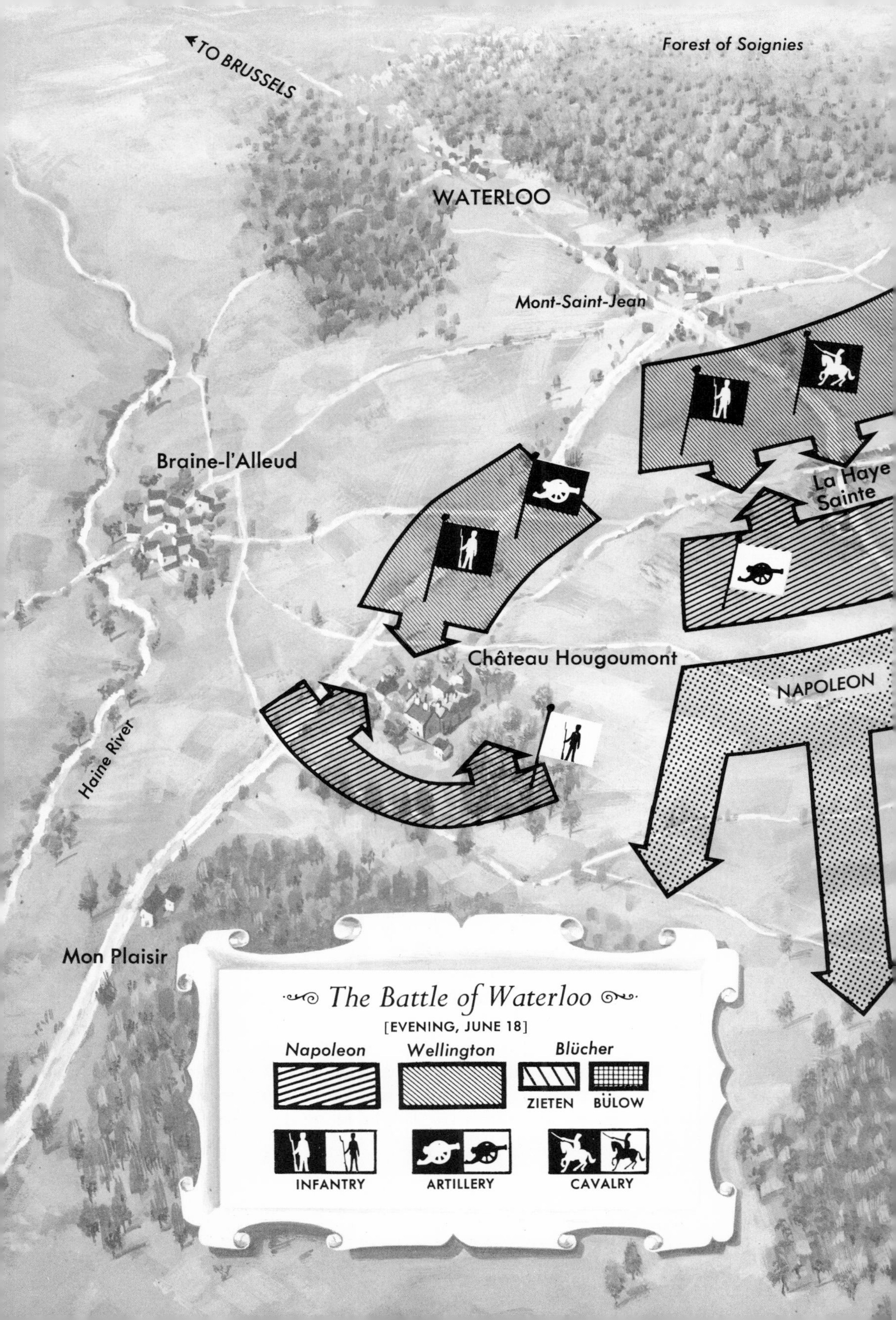

TO BRUSSELS

Forest of Soignies

WATERLOO

Mont-Saint-Jean

Braine-l'Alleud

La Haye
Sainte

NAPOLEON

Château Hougoumont

Haine River

Mon Plaisir

The Battle of Waterloo
[EVENING, JUNE 18]

Napoleon	Wellington	Blücher	
		ZIETEN	BÜLOW

INFANTRY	ARTILLERY	CAVALRY

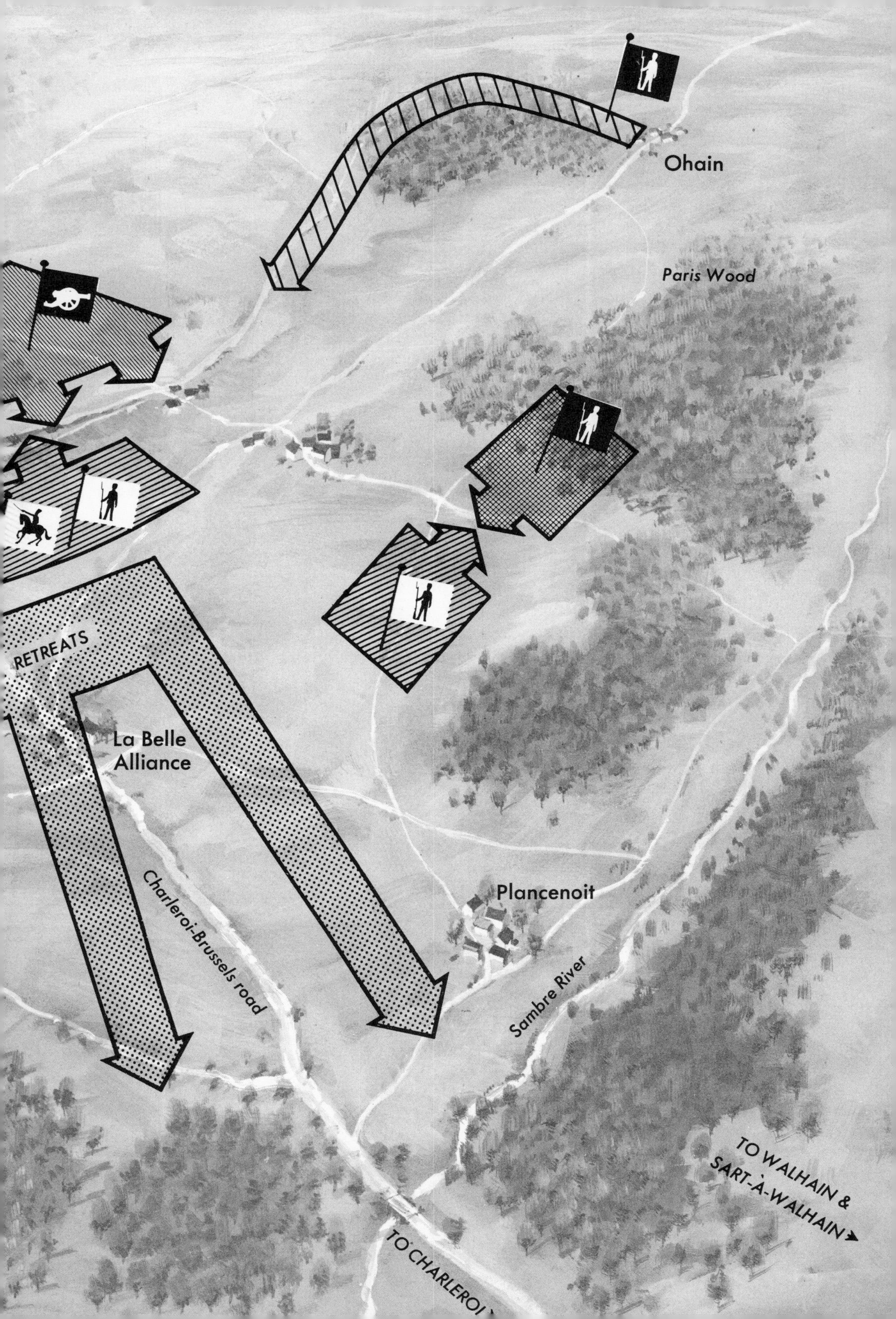

Ohain

Paris Wood

RETREATS

La Belle
Alliance

Plancenoit

Charleroi-Brussels road

Sambre River

TO WALHAIN &
SART-À-WALHAIN ➤

TO CHARLEROI

closed again. French troops are badly beaten attempting to assault
the fortress.

The movement is badly directed in every respect. Jerome has
scanty knowledge of the enemy position. Artillery is used at the
wrong time and in the wrong way.

12:30 P.M. British reinforcements strengthen the fortress.
Jerome, not realizing his operation has been intended only as a diversion, pours wave after wave of troops against Hougoumont to
be killed or repulsed.

At about the same time, Napoleon preludes the attack on Wellington's left center, the main thrust, with a cannonade from eighty-
four guns. The British guns reply and a furious artillery duel rages.
Wellington's infantry are partly sheltered from the intense bombardment. They are in the "Wellington position," just behind the
brow of the ridge where the guns are placed.

1:00 P.M. Napoleon prepares to order Ney's assault on La Haye
Sainte. But taking a last look around, he notices what looks like a
thick black cloud coming out of the woods of Chapelle Saint
Lambert, to the northeast. A hasty reconnaissance verifies the sus-
picion that it is Bülow's corps of 30,000 Prussians advancing on the
French right flank. Twelve hours too late, Napoleon sends a dispatch
to Grouchy, finally ordering him to come at once, then says: "This
morning we had ninety chances in our favor. Even now we have
sixty chances, and only forty against us."

1:30 P.M. Napoleon sends Lobau to head off Bülow with 10,000
men, thus diminishing his main force by that number. He then
orders Ney to open the attack on Wellington's center with D'Erlon.
After an hour and a half of steady firing, the cannons stop to permit
the troops to advance.

Ney and D'Erlon have made two bad mistakes: (1) The troops
have advanced in columns, an extremely clumsy formation which
does not permit proper deployment when the enemy is encountered.
Even where the French muskets outnumber the British near the top
of the hill, their firepower is not usable, since only the narrow
front ranks are able to shoot. (2) Vital cavalry support has not been
used until much too late.

Also, because of the "Wellington position," the French bombardment has not done the usual job of softening up. The French
troops have been driven back to their original position. However,
the British Union Brigade has been practically wiped out.

2:30 P.M. Château Hougoumont, under increased French cannon fire, bursts into flames. But still the British there hold out.

3.00 P.M. Napoleon receives a dispatch from Grouchy, written at 11:00 from Walhain, that he is heading for Wavre. This should force Napoleon to realize that he must forget about help from Grouchy on the 18th.

3:30 P.M. Napoleon orders Ney to storm La Haye Sainte. No heavy guns are used to batter down the walls in advance of the infantry charge. The attack fails.

4:00 P.M. Napoleon, more and more concerned about the appearance of the Prussians, turns over most of the responsibility for the main attack to Ney—one more mistake in the assignment of high-command positions. Ney, originally a cavalry officer, decides to assault the British center with cavalry alone. The leading squadrons are blown apart by the British guns. The British infantry forms into squares, covering the ground like a chessboard, entangling the French cavalry. Then the British cavalry charges and drives the French back. French artillery, which would have provided valuable support for the attack, is not used to advantage.

4:30 P.M. Lobau, detached to stop or slow down Bülow's Prussians on the right, makes the mistake of failing to engage them inside the Paris Wood, where the fight would have delayed the Prussians. Out in the open, Lobau is able to keep them back only for a short time.

5:30 P.M. Napoleon orders a fresh charge of cavalry against Wellington's center, thereby using up all his heavy reserves. Again he fails to provide infantry and artillery support for the attack. In the ensuing fight, Wellington is forced to use up his reserves, too, and better French tactics might have won Napoleon a decisive victory at this moment.

5:45 P.M. Bülow pushes Lobau back and back and captures Plancenoit, threatening Napoleon's line of retreat.

6:00 P.M. Ney, with the remnants of D'Erlon's corps, finally captures La Haye Sainte when the garrison there runs out of ammunition.

7:00 P.M. The Old Guard, hurrying to Plancenoit, drives out the Prussians.

7:30 P.M. The showdown has arrived. Wellington's main line is badly weakened. Part of D'Erlon's corps has gained the top of Wellington's ridge. The French have captured La Haye Sainte and recaptured Plancenoit. If he is ever to do so, this is the time for Napoleon to crush the Anglo-Dutch Army. To bolster morale, Napoleon spreads the word among his troops that Grouchy is close at hand.

But while the French rally after capturing La Haye Sainte, Wellington receives valuable reinforcements from the rear. And a great number of French soldiers are still at Plancenoit, a mile and a half away. A French cavalry officer deserts and warns Wellington of the nature of Napoleon's planned attack, allowing the British to make the appropriate countermoves in advance.

SUNSET.   In an all-out move, Napoleon hurls three great waves against two points in Wellington's line.

8:00 P.M.   But the French are repulsed, though the Old Guard fights bitterly. At this moment a large Prussian detachment under Zieten strikes the northeastern side of the French front and caves it in. This is the decisive blow. With the exception of two battalions of the Old Guard, the French Army breaks apart and flees.

Meanwhile, Bülow recaptures Plancenoit. The French troops there under Lobau move back to guard the Charleroi road for Napoleon's retreat.

9:15 P.M.   Wellington and Blücher meet at La Belle Alliance and decide the Prussians should pursue Napoleon. As darkness settles over the bloody landscape, illumined only by the burning of Plancenoit in the distance, Wellington says, "I have never fought such a battle, and I trust I shall never fight such another."

During the night the Prussians force Napoleon out of one bivouac after the next, until he is out of Belgium.

EVENTS FOLLOWING WATERLOO

MONDAY, JUNE 19, 5:00 A.M.   Napoleon reaches Charleroi.

9:00 A.M.   Napoleon reaches Philippeville. Grouchy is retreating through Namur to Gembloux. But the Prussians stay in pursuit. They reach Charleroi on the 19th, Avesnes on the 22nd, Saint-Germain on July 1st, and Versailles on July 3rd. Wellington is close behind.

JULY 7.   The Allies march into Paris.

JULY 8.   Louis XVIII is back on the throne of France.

Ney, leading the remains of D'Erlon's reserves, meets fierce resistance from Wellington's infantry at La Haye Sainte on the strategic Charleroi-Brussels road. (Engraving by Sutherland)

Blücher Supports Wellington

Wellington's center was now greatly weakened. His troops were exhausted and his reserves already used up. And although the Iron Duke with bulldog tenacity quickly began to reorganize his forces, Napoleon held an edge over him for the first time during that long day.

Napoleon, however, was unable to press the advantage he held because two more of Blücher's corps now arrived to aid Wellington. One unit of 32,500 men and cavalry and 96 cannons was under the command of Zieten and the other was under George D. L. Pirch.

Pirch's corps, numbering 32,500 men and cavalry and 80 cannons, joined Bülow in Paris Wood, and together they immediately launched an attack on Napoleon's right flank. The Young Guard, with its artillery, engaged them in fierce and bloody fighting. But it was unable to check their advance, and the Prussians soon captured the village of Plancenoit, which was behind the French lines.

Napoleon immediately sent out two battalions of the Old Guard. Plancenoit must be recaptured at any cost.

The hand-to-hand fighting which followed was gory and bestial. The battle raged in the cemetery and through the narrow village streets. The burning houses bathed the combatants in scorching heat.

With Plancenoit once more in French hands, Napoleon ordered a massive attack against the entire length of Wellington's line. But he had acted too late. With the arrival of the Prussians, Wellington had been able to reinforce his weak center with two cavalry brigades from his left flank. Now their joint forces greatly outnumbered the French.

When Napoleon learned of this, he decided on one last desperate act. Believing he heard Grouchy's gunfire, he thought he must be close at hand. Grouchy's 33,000 fresh men could save the day! He summoned forward the remaining four battalions of his faithful Old Guard, the "Old Grumblers" as he affectionately called them. Placing himself at their head, he led them to La Haye Sainte, the little farm just won at the cost of so many thousands of lives.

Standing in a cloud of battle smoke, Napoleon addressed the Old Guard between the boom of cannons. He stirred them deeply with his oratory, secretly sending messengers into their midst to announce the approach of Marshal Grouchy, so that they might believe that victory was near. Then he handed them over to Marshal Ney.

Meanwhile, Grouchy had involved himself in a useless,

The Old Guard in close combat near the village of Plancenoit

drawn-out battle over a bridge in Wavre, rejecting his officers' advice to join the main fighting at Waterloo. As a result, when Napoleon's imperative order finally reached him, Grouchy was blocked from moving westward at all.

The Old Guard

The brave and battle-hardened men of the Old Guard were moved by the Emperor's words to renewed determination. But Wellington's forces, recognizing their famous big bearskin hats from the distance and knowing them to be savage fighters, determined to show them no mercy. They directed the fire of all their available cannons into the Old Guard's midst.

So heavy was the smoke that for a time the Old Guard was lost from sight. But then Wellington's men heard them shouting "Vive l'Empereur!" and knew that the charge was on. Suddenly the smoke cleared and the French were close at hand, line upon line of flashing bayonets.

"Fire!" Wellington's officers gave the command.

In less than a minute, three hundred of the Old Guard were lying dead or wounded on the ground.

Seeing this, an English captain called out, "Now's the time, my boys!" And his brigade sprang forward for a hand-to-hand encounter with those veteran "Old Grumblers."

Another battalion of the Old Guard was seen approaching through the heavy battle smoke. It was the voice of Welling-

Wellington, on Copenhagen, gallops along the front line, urging his men forward for the final pursuit of Napoleon's French Army.

ton himself that was heard calling out, "Now! Now's your time!" A volley of rifle fire and cannon grapeshot scattered this second charge.

After the battle smoke had again cleared, more dead and wounded covered the ground. And Marshal Ney, his uniform cut and torn, could be seen staggering about with a broken sword in his hand, shouting and urging the men forward. His horse had been shot from under him.

Neither of these French charges had been supported on the flanks by cavalry or infantry. And so the great Old Guard, which until now had known only victories, faced defeat. To add to their disaster, Zieten and his corps of 32,500 men, cavalry, and cannons now launched a new attack on the French right flank.

The Old Guard still fought on. Ney kept pouring more and more troops into the inferno along the entire line. But with every passing minute it became more evident that he could not keep this up much longer. And at 8:00 P.M., when the Prussians smashed through the French right, the whole French line crumbled.

Wellington, still riding Copenhagen, now galloped along his front. Waving his hat, he shouted his now famous words, "The whole line will advance!" He gave the signal to press forward.

Wellington knew the battle was won. But this was not enough. He was determined to annihilate Napoleon. To make this Napoleon's final battle, he had to wipe out the whole French Army. With this end in view, Wellington's entire line left the ridge and, with a great clamor, flags flying, drums beating, bagpipes piping, bands playing, streamed down into what only that morning had been beautiful fields of new green wheat.

Defeat

These fields were now the scene of panic. The French infantry, cavalry, and artillery had lost all semblance of order and position. They merged pell-mell into one great seething mass. Some of the most loyal were trying to hold their formations and fight the oncoming enemy. Others, whole squares, were attempting an orderly retreat. But the great mass were bent on fleeing as best they could.

Clouds of low-lying smoke enveloped sections of the field. Bullets and cannon balls still whined in the air. The ground was strewn with the remains of battle; it was covered with shattered cannons and gun carriages. The mangled bodies of dead and wounded men lay jumbled together. The litter told its own story: plumed helmets, gaiters, drums, sabers, dead horses, shoes, boots, knapsacks, metal breastplates, shakos, bearskin hats, mess bowls, knives and forks, cannon balls, lances, torns bits of gold braid, epaulets, bagpipes, bugles, trumpets, and flags.

Through this wreckage Wellington's forces now pushed their way, determined to grind the remaining French into the ground. This time they would make sure that the French defeat was complete.

Napoleon was brilliant in victory, but he could not stand defeat. In the confusion and panic that prevailed on the battlefield, he did not know which way to turn. He was deathly pale, his face wet with tears. He staggered from exhaustion. He had taken a good deal of snuff, and his head was swimming as he called to his aides, "Now it is all over. Let us get away."

The panic was on now; it was each man for himself. This was true even for Napoleon, Emperor of France. Afraid of

Retreat of the French from Waterloo (Painting by A. C. Gow)

being captured, for one brief period he took refuge in the hollow of one of his retreating squares. Once off the battlefield, he fled on horseback toward Quatre Bras.

At 9:15 P.M. Wellington and Blücher met at La Belle Alliance. They did not dismount, but old Blücher leaned over and kissed the Iron Duke. Speaking of the battle, he said in French, *"Quelle affaire!"* ("What a business!")

Doom

At 1:00 A.M. Napoleon was in Quatre Bras. At 6:00 A.M. he was in Charleroi. It was now exactly one week since his carriage had rolled rapidly out of Paris in the dead of night, headed for the Belgian border.

At that time, he dreamed of parading triumphantly through

Brussels and of victory over all the kings of Europe. And now . . . He had left his carriage at his battle headquarters and his sword was on the seat. Both the carriage and the sword were in enemy hands.

The Battle of Waterloo was over, a battle whose outcome was so decisive that to this day the word "Waterloo" is used to designate complete disaster. But even at that late hour the pursuit of the French was not abandoned. Seven times during the night their fast-retreating armies tried to make camp, and seven times the enemy was upon them. They could find no rest. The British and their Allies were determined to drive Napoleon all the way back to Paris and then to occupy that ancient and beautiful city. Only the dead on a field soaked with blood had rest. Scattered here and there in the mud lay the colorful parade uniforms which had fallen from torn knapsacks.

The French had lost over 40,000 men; the English, 15,000; and the Prussians, 7,000. In all, the battle had cost the lives of 62,000 men. In fact, the fighting had been so desperate that when the sun went down on that historic Sunday at Waterloo there was a three-square-mile area of the battlefield on which lay over 45,000 dead and wounded!

Adding the dead at Waterloo to those at Quatre Bras and Ligny, the staggering total of men slaughtered in two days of fighting was 91,800.

Two days later Napoleon was in Paris. His defeat was bitter. For the second time in two years, invading armies were closing in about the French capital.

Was this the end for Napoleon? Perhaps not. The Emperor had still another plan. . . . But the Minister of War, Davout, appointed by Napoleon, refused to place the remaining shreds of the French Army in his hands.

In the Chamber of Deputies, an old son of freedom rose to speak. He was La Fayette, loyal friend of Washington, Jefferson, and Franklin. "I can see only one man between us and peace," he said. "If we rid ourselves of him, peace will be ours for the asking."

The victors, Wellington and Blücher, at La Belle Alliance (Detail from an engraving after a painting by Daniel Maclise)

These words sealed Napoleon's doom. On Thursday, June 22, 1815, he abdicated for the second time, thus ending the "Hundred Days," the period from the night he entered Paris and reassumed his crown until the day he gave up his authority. And on Sunday, June 25th, just one week after the Battle of Waterloo, Napoleon left Paris, never to return.

A few days later Napoleon was at the Channel port of Rochefort, seeking a ship to carry him to America. The English, however, did not intend to let him escape. Several of their cruisers blocked the harbor.

To add to Napoleon's difficulties, the provisional government of Paris now gave him twenty-four hours to leave French soil. Confronted with this ultimatum, Napoleon decided to throw himself upon the generosity of the British. Not realizing how much they hated him, he wrote a personal letter of appeal to the English King, asking to be granted asylum in England. Then he mounted the deck of H.M.S.

Bellerophon which was in the harbor and surrendered to its master, Captain Maitland.

His hopes were quickly crushed. His letter was never answered. The *Bellerophon* sailed at once to Portsmouth, where he was transferred to a British man-of-war.

The Dying Embers

On the day following the Battle of Waterloo, as dawn brought light once more to the bloody field, men and women could be seen wandering over the battleground. Some were sightseers; others were scavengers robbing the dead. Still others were parents, children, wives, and other close relatives seeking those they loved.

An Englishwoman, Lady de Lancey, found her young husband lying wounded among the dead. She managed to have him carried to a house in a nearby village where she

nursed him tenderly. However, he died and she returned alone to England. Her diary ends with these touching words: "It is exactly one month ago today that we were married." That the English had "won" made little difference to her and thousands like her.

A French soldier, who had somehow remained behind, picked up a newborn baby girl abandoned upon the field. How she got there no one knew. He took her home and raised her lovingly. When she grew to womanhood, she and the soldier were married. Years later her granddaughter became the wife of the elderly Ferdinand de Lesseps, the engineer who built the Suez Canal.

After Napoleon's abdication, the hated King, Louis XVIII, returned to Paris and once more mounted the throne of France. He ruled for nine years after Waterloo before he died.

Marshal Ney, the "bravest of the brave," died before a firing squad—shot as a traitor to the King.

Marshal Blücher, "Old Forwards," enjoyed the victory celebrations in Paris and then returned to his estate in Prussia, where he died four years later.

Wellington became England's hero. In gratitude, Parliament voted him a present of 200,000 pounds, which equaled about one million dollars. It also bestowed upon him the title, "Prince of Waterloo."

And Copenhagen? He was rewarded by being retired to the green fields on Wellington's estate. When he finally died, Wellington had bracelets and rings made of his tail and mane, and presented them as mementos of the Battle of Waterloo to the pretty young girls and charming ladies of his acquaintance.

And what of the military hero who had once conquered

most of Europe? The British man-of-war carried Napoleon
Bonaparte to St. Helena, a black, craggy island a thousand
miles west of the southern coast of Africa. There he lived
in a lonely, bitter exile, a victim of his own disregard for
human life. Six years later Napoleon Bonaparte died.

Napoleon boards the British ship Bellerophon,
headed for England and exile.

*The defeated Master of Europe in final exile on the island of
St. Helena, where he died in 1821. (Lithograph by C. Fuhr)*

Napoleon's Army of the North (Armée du Nord)

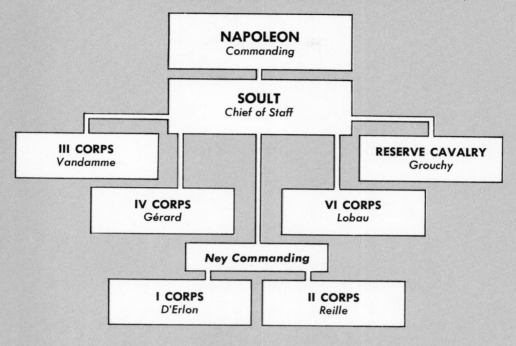

Allied Armies

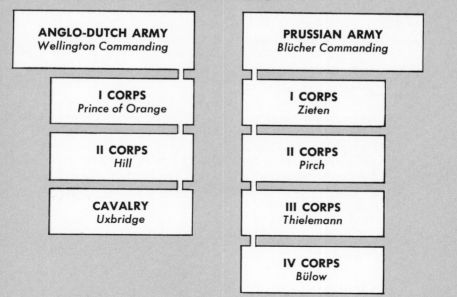

FOR FURTHER READING

Nonfiction

BELL, DOUGLAS H. *Wellington's Officers*. London: Collins, 1938.

FISHER, HERBERT A. L. *Napoleon*. New York: Oxford University Press, 1945.

GUÉRARD, ALBERT L. *Napoleon I*. New York: Knopf, 1956.

KIRCHEISEN, FRIEDRICH M. *Napoleon*. New York: Harcourt, Brace, 1932.

*KOMROFF, MANUEL. *Napoleon*. New York: Messner, 1954.

LOCKHART, JOHN G. *The History of Napoleon Bonaparte*. New York: Dutton, 1915.

LUDWIG, EMIL. *Napoleon*. New York: Modern Library.

NAPOLEON I. *The Waterloo Campaign*. Translated and edited by Somerset De Chair, London: Folio Society, 1957.

NAYLOR, JOHN. *Waterloo*. New York: Macmillan, 1960.

RATCLIFFE, BERTRAM. *Marshal de Grouchy and the Guns of Waterloo*. London: Muller, 1942.

THOMPSON, JAMES M. *Napoleon Bonaparte: His Rise and Fall*. New York: Oxford University Press, 1952.

*WINWAR, FRANCES. *Napoleon and the Battle of Waterloo*. New York: Random, 1953.

Fiction

CHAMBERS, ROSAMUND M. *Strangers at the Farm*. London: Cassell, 1961.

ERCKMANN, EMILE (translator). *Waterloo* and *The Conscript of 1813* (from the French of Erckmann-Chatrian). New York: Scribners, 1912.

KOMROFF, MANUEL. *Waterloo*. New York: Coward-McCann, 1936.

ROTH, JOSEPH. *The Ballad of the Hundred Days*. New York: Viking, 1936.

* Books for young readers

INDEX